YOUNG THIEVES IN A GROWING ORCHARD

SHORT STORIES

SAMUEL E. COLE

Weasel Press

Young Thieves in a Growing Orchard
Samuel E. Cole

ISBN: 978-1-948712-26-2

Young Thieves in a Growing Orchard © 2019 Samuel E. Cole
Cover Design by Nicole Bundy

https://www.samuel-cole.com/

Weasel Press
Manvel, TX
www.weaselpress.com

Printed in the U.S.A.

Contents

Special thanks to Weasel Press for believing in this collection, Nicole Bundy for designing the front cover, spine, and back cover, Jeffrey Whitney for cheering my voice, and to the feedback dispensing members of The Minneapolis Writers Workshop.

For all those who wish to belong

Young Thieves in a Growing Orchard

DOROTHY DAY & HAMMOND NIGHT

The shower animates my body, water pellets releasing dull layers of chapped skin peeling beneath patches of straight black hair and purple warts of which I understand neither the origin nor the longevity. Wrinkles and age spots embossing my face stretch in the oval mirror like rows of useless dirt. A toothbrush and toothpaste do little to remove the brown film coating my teeth, nor relieve the pain of gum loss receding to an upper lip. I have not been kind to myself. And it shows. People, even nuns, wince at my appearance: a trailing beard with four braids tied off with red rubber bands; green eyes that have darkened into ominousness; fingernails bitten to the cuticle; a distended belly on account of sodium-laden shelter food, cheap, stolen beer from affluent trashcans, and reused syringes from the ghettos of Minneapolis and Saint Paul. I was fresh once. And spoiled. For two years. Twenty to twenty-two years of age. A time when plenty filled in the skeletons of a cracked past, when want replaced need, when fitting in tempted me to overestimate the allure of permanency. My parents told me that lavishness was beyond their, and my, grasp. And they were right.

The bath towel smells of the lakefront summer mornings

when I lived with Hammond Anderson. Nineteen years my senior, Hammond who was a financial consultant for Citibank, revealed retirement funds on a second date, after a rodeo, after I asked why a man needs two cars, two estates, two retirement funds, two horses, two cats.

"Did you grow up poor?" he asked.

"I grew up understanding confines."

"That sounds limiting."

"Life is a series of limitations."

"What if I could help change that?"

"I live in a friend's garage and ride a bike to work," I said. "I don't get change."

"Is that a yes or a no?"

"I have never wished for things beyond my grasp."

He pointed to the total column at the bottom of the retirement funds: $703, 231.00 "How does seeing this make you feel?"

"Is that a real amount?"

"Feel a little less poor now?"

"It's not mine."

He smiled. "You're young and hung. You've got it all."

Fists banging on the bathroom door turn my attention back to a red-orange face and coffee breath fogging the mirror.

"Hurry up in there, I ain't got all day," a voice yells.

I stuff the baby-sized toiletries into a plastic bag, sleeve and leg a gray sweat suit, tie white shoelaces, and open the door.

"About time," a young man says, bumping my shoulder as he takes the bathroom, slamming the door. "Fucking queer."

"Hi, Mister Eloc," Hunter, the volunteer coordinator, says, holding a clipboard. "You smell amaze."

"Lavender body wash and ocean-scented lotion."

"You gonna be here for dinner tonight?"

"Always and forever."

"Got a new volunteer team from a bank coming in to serve and I was hoping you might tour 'em."

"Sure."

"Amaze." He smiles. Bright teeth. Symmetrical and luminous. "They're coming in to prepare food about four o'clock. Maybe you can meet them before dinner, if there's time, or maybe after."

I nod, spotting a seat at a small table in the left corner of the room, a place for those who shower, sit, read, and stare at their own hands. A homeless shelter is like high school—there's a lot of cliques who keep to themselves and there's a lot of opinions who don't.

"This table's full," Ed the Sniffler says, scooting an empty chair with a bare foot into the table.

Sandra the Overcoat laughs, and sings, "Tables full. Tables full. Tables, tables, tables full."

Jacob the Dead Eyes slaps shut a book and yells, "This is the silent area. Be quiet or get the hell out."

"Quiet area. Quiet area. Quiet, quiet, quiet area."

"Sssssssshhhhhh." Jacob turns his back on Ed and Sandra and opens the book. "Good god, you bunch a weirdos."

I scan the room for another place to sit. There's an empty table near the toiletry desk. And for good reason. Anyone who sits there gets badgered by the staff to volunteer. Same reason the table in front of the washer and dryer is empty. As is the table near the clothes closet. Here, for most clients, to give is not better than to receive. I stand to the left of the front door and wait for the bitchy front desk lady to call out and hand out tickets for dinner. I'm usually number one to ten, mostly because I've memorized the food schedule but also because Hunter looks out for me, reminding the front desk staff to make sure I get a ticket. I believe he likes me. He acts like he likes me. Perhaps it is an act, an obligation as an employee to be kind to the desolate and downcast. Or perhaps it's because I shower and never complain about the thin-trickle water faucets, the ill-lit bathrooms, and the cushionless cot I'm made to sleep on overnight. I'd be fucked if I had a bad back. Or maybe he's nice because I agree to give tours to new volunteer groups who wear nice clothes with combed hair who look at me, as I talk about The Dorothy Day Center, as if I'm the most interesting, and most disgusting, person in the world. Last week, a young girl asked if I was a client or a volunteer.

"I'm a client volunteer," I said.

"So, you live here day and night?"

"I do indeed."

"But it smells so bad and there's no color on the walls."

I chuckled. "I provide the smell and the color, because I am the walls."

Dinner in the cafeteria is another version of lukewarm meatloaf and strawberry Kool-Aid. A few volunteers bring stale cookies and brownies to the tables. Some of them smile and squat as if they're talking to, and placating, toddlers. Most of them stay behind the serving line, a long row of metal hot plates that serve as a barrier between our illness and their health, our folly and their sanity, our collapse and their gain. No one asks for a name, even when I offer it. Which isn't often. I don't believe in public-exhibitionism. I do, however, believe there are do-gooders who do good in order to hide the bad they don't want others to see, others like us at The Dorothy Day Center, who because we cannot hide, must be bad, you see.

Hunter comes to the table and squats. "Ready to tour the new group?"

"Always and forever."

"Amaze." He stands. "I'll send them to the conference

room in ten or fifteen minutes, after the other clients go outside. The room's unlocked. Make yourself at home until they get there."

"That I can do."

"You're a gem, Mr. Eloc." He touches my forearm. His whisper titillates my right ear. He smells of youth and peaches. Wetness enlivens his lips and skin. Blue eyes the stuff of splendor. Hands and ass the size of raging lust. "We're so lucky to have you."

Lucky to have me. Yes, dear Hunter, you can. Anytime. I am yours.

The conference room fills with fellow Caucasians chatting about how good they feel in their servanthood and how they wish to do it again. Soon. I stand in the front and hold out my hands. A quick hush overtakes the room. If I hold any power in the universe, it's in this moment. The old homeless guy is about to speak so shut up and listen or else he might pull out a knife from that gross beard and stab us, everyone.

"I hope you enjoyed the volunteer experience."

They nod and look quizzically at each other, as if they're unsure whether to be astounded by the coherent sentence or confused that I'm able to deliver it without spittle drooling down the side of my mouth. I often wonder the reaction if I spun in circles and rippled a tongue-shrill on the roof my mouth. I want to try it, but I fear the action will turn counter-intuition into counter-production. I'd be sad if I lost the task of giving tours, and I do not wish, ever, to disappoint Hunter.

"Before we go on the tour, does anyone have any questions?"

"Are you a client?"

"I'm a client volunteer."

"So, you live here day and night?"

"I do indeed."

A portly man in a grey suit enters the room, stands in the back, and taps lightly a shiny, black shoe against the wall. The other volunteers sitting around the table nod and wave. He smiles and gives two thumbs up. Experience tells me he's either a bigwig who hires and fires or a small wig who's making a move to the top in order to hire and fire. Suits don't serve the meal; suits come in later and write the donation check to the Development Department. Hunter was the first staffer to clue me in on these facts, on his second day of work, right after I gave him a tour.

"What's your position in the company?" the portly man asks. He sounds like Hammond Anderson, but he looks like a creampuff with scarecrow hair. Not like Hammond at all.

"I'm a client volunteer."

"A what?"

"A client volunteer."

"So you're served by this place while you serve this place."

I nod.

"Are you happy here?"

I stand quiet for a few seconds, staring at my hands. "I am of service here and that brings me a certain degree of peace and belonging."

"Ah," he says. "Please continue."

"Dorothy Day was born on November 8, 1897 and lived until November 29, 1980," I say. "She was an American journalist, social activist, and Catholic convert. She initially lived a bohemian lifestyle before gaining fame as a social activist after her conversion. She later became a key figure in the Catholic Worker Movement and earned a national reputation as a political radical, perhaps the most famous radical in American Catholic Church history."

"I thought we were gonna tour the facility," the portly

man says.

"We will, but I like to start off with a bit about the woman, Dorothy Day."

"We all have lives to get to, so perhaps we can skip the upsell."

"Whatever you want." I walk to and open the French doors. The crowd stands and follows my narration around the facility, stopping in front of The Healthcare for the Homeless Clinic, Direct Services, Employment Assistance, Housing Support, The Food Shelf, The Warehouse, the Upstairs Bunk Bed Area for Women, and the Downstairs Cot Room for Men. Lots of ooh's and ah's, wide eyes skimming the contents of the rooms, privileged pupils looking upon things beyond their everyday.

"Thanks for coming to volunteer. Drive safe and please consider volunteering again."

Most of the crowd departs through the back door. The portly man stays behind, writing in front of Hunter what looks like a check. I stand by the back door, wondering which snack and soda Hunter has waiting for us in the kitchen as payment for my service. He likes Doritos and Coke, so that's usually the fare.

"What's the tour guides name?" the portly man asks Hunter.

"We're not allowed to give out personal information, but feel free to ask him yourself." Hunter turns and smiles at me. "He wants to meet you, wants to know your name."

I nod.

"Come over."

I walk toward Hunter, longing for his arms, for one embrace, for one moment to soak in loveliness no mirror has ever reflected. He's young, and I choose to believe he's hung. His tight shininess makes me question whether he understands how quickly age and frailty show up and destroy the fantasy of spent radiance. The portly man has a strong hand shake. Like Hammond's hand shake. He pulls me toward him as if to inspect damaged goods.

"What's your name?" he asks.

"Just call me friend."

"Do you have a first name?"

I nod.

"Well, what is it?"

I look at Hunter.

"It's up to you, if you want to tell him."

I look into the portly man's eyes. Green like Hammond. Clear like Hammond. Menacing like Hammond. But he can't be Hammond. Hammond was lean. Hammond was hazel. Hammond was so long ago. Twenty-three years. Two of every season followed by a yellow eviction notice. Go. Get. Leave me alone, you loser. That's the last time you're gonna steal my credit card for drugs, you trailer trash, and overdose my niece, you rotten scumbag. I knew better than to get involved with your type of nothingness. A mistake I will correct and never make again. Now get the fuck out of my house.

"I hope you enjoyed the tour, sir."

"Is that you, Leumas?" he asks.

"You've got the wrong guy."

"It's you, isn't it?"

"My name's Phil." I lie, still able to recall the numbers on his credit card, a MasterCard, with a thousand dollar cash advance, and a signature scrawled with highs and lows of which I took advantage and ignored the consequences. I turn and walk toward the kitchen.

"I swear it's him," Hammond tells Hunter. "I swear it."

"I can't reveal personal information, sir. I'm sorry."

"But I know him. Knew him. I'm telling you, I know who he is."

"Thanks for volunteering tonight. Drive safe and please consider volunteering again."

"I know who you are," Hammond yells at my back. "And this young man should know what it is that you did."

In the kitchen, I lean against the dishwasher, a first job at Dorothy Day Center so long ago, before the beard, the wrinkles, the age spots, and Hunter, the very day I told a taxi driver to drop me and my plastic bags off at the closest homeless shelter—183 Old Sixth Street Saint Paul, MN 55102.

Final Leg Home

Sailboat captains dream of days like today: breezy, seventy five degrees, sunny, and three, prepaid, packed island tours. If forty years of commandeering *The Lords and Ladies* has taught me anything, it's that one beautiful Saturday can pay for a week of rainy Tuesdays, balmy Fridays, and football Sundays. If I were a praying man, I'd thank God. If I smiled, I'd show gums. Instead, I open sails, restock beer, polish brass, scrub decks, iron uniforms, dust hats, and spit-shine black dress shoes with white laces. Obligations that must be fulfilled before I can welcome, and decode for possible feeding, the next batch of payees.

Below the deck, to maintain a human appearance, I finish off Mr. Polamalu's thigh and wipe the juice from my mouth with his girlfriend's right hand. Polamalu was a lean, muscular triathlete. His girlfriend, may she rest juicily in the refrigerator, was a gold medal bodybuilder. (I feel like a rapper whenever I hang the gold medal around my neck, which I haven't done in a few weeks. Not out of respect, but from a never-ending fatigue I am tired of carrying.)

Being the thoughtful, living death I have to portray—no thanks to Captain Ellsworth before me, who affixed me to this vessel by way of a whisper, an incantation I can't remember, into a drunken ear—I spray the cabin, and myself, with lemon scented Febreze. Human's tip better when things smell, and look, alive, and I can ill-afford to lose tens, twenties, or fifties, if I'm lucky, as gas prices alone have skyrocketed a hundred-fold. I'd be sunk if not for full-service helpfulness via smartphone.

Polamalu and his girlfriend's surrender, albeit an unwilling one, came at a period of low-to-no-tour desperation. I had a glove for a left hand, a tennis shoe for a left foot, and an eye-patch over an empty, left socket. "Three square meals a day," Captain Ellsworth said, "Or things will get really, really ugly." Then he vanished, leaving me to bleed without blood.

The stateroom mirror confirms my handsomeness. I look better now than I did on my wedding day, when I had pockmarked skin and a balding pate, and my wife, Lady Helena, who Captain Ellsworth devoured in front of me, had motion and morning sickness.

Helena had begged me to postpone the sailboat excursion. But I didn't. Instead, I manipulated her with honeymoon words about a romantic cruise around the Apostle Islands which may never come our way again, and also how much we'd regret missing the opportunity.

I tap my cheeks and finger-slope my neck.

Polamalu and his girlfriend have done their job quite well. Trouble is, I'm always peeling. And, I'm tired. And, the pursuit of gathering more and more grows less and less satisfying. I long to bring to sunset sunrises that hold only greed and consumption. If I could only remember the incantation, find an ear in which to whisper its confines, gain freedom, and vanish. The clock chimes 9am, and for a moment, its purpose uplifts my head to follow a patch of clouds drifting with solace through the ether.

The first tour is my least favorite. Three gay couples

with overdressed Chihuahuas hop aboard. "Hold on tight, cuz I don't turn back for dogs." I scan their bodies but decide to pass. I don't eat meth or STDs, but since gay men are good tippers, I narrate backstory details of, and around, the biggest island, which is also the first stop-and-drop of the day.

"Stay well," I say, accepting three, twenty dollar bills, "And be safe," I add for comedic effect. They laugh and pat me on the back. Gay men, I've learned, have a high tolerance for sarcastic insinuation.

The second tour to the next island is the longest and loudest. Four identical toddlers with head lice, a thin-skinned woman, and a hefty man come aboard and play, for fifteen minutes, musical chairs and the scream-till-I-get-my-way game. I neither point out the life jackets nor narrate historical facts. I forgo mentioning bottled water and snacks. Stepping off, they don't offer a smile, a thank you, or cash. In that moment, I wish to nibble on a toddler ear, but I don't, won't, and can't eat babies.

The two-hour lapse between the second stop and the last trek to evening-anchor affords the opportunity to gnaw on Polamalu's girlfriend. After a couple of bites of shoulder tendons, I can crack knuckles and knees without detachment. After a mouthful of fresh lung, my vision is ten-ten. The large intestine makes me feel better than alive, but alert and refreshed, everything working as it should, curling hairline to a reduction of plantar fasciitis.

The clock chimes 5:30pm and tomorrow is closer than farther away, with another packed itinerary with me at the helm. I fear my late wife and unnamed baby — I call her Lady Junebug — whose grandchildren's shadows dance and sing around my bed, will fade even further than pixilation. Then who will I be?

Six, twenty-something girls jump aboard at 6pm.

"Welcome. I'm Captain Blade."

"Your hat's super sex," the unhealthiest girl says, pushing a finger into my chest. She grabs the hat and puts it on a red head. "Ready to give me the ride of my life, I hope."

"You have no idea." I turn on the overhead lights, open the mini-bar, and crank up the radio. Of the six, the most promising meal is an energetic, long-haired brunette the other girls call Cindy. She keeps staring at me as is she wants to eat me. She craves attention, which I'm more than willing to give. My tongue, like the wind, is strong. I wet my lips and ask, "So, where ya from?"

"Go, Bruno the Bear," they cheer in unison.

Bruno the Bear is the Brown University mascot. Captain Ellsworth collected encyclopedias, and I'm a ferocious reader. I give two thumbs up, excited to dine with, and on, ivy-league boob. I can almost lick Cindy's dirty thoughts.

"Where's the bathroom on this pleasure cruiser?" Cindy asks, twisting hair into a ponytail.

I set the sails, takeoff, and nod downstairs. "Have at it."

"Care to join me?" she asks, taking a first step down. Her friends giggle, blow air kisses, and wish us a delish-commish. Two of the girls complain about the lack of cell phone reception, while the unhealthiest girl takes the wheel, and says, "My dad has a sailboat, so I got this, dude."

Downstairs, I lock the bathroom door and remove my vest. Cindy's already on her knees.

"Don't worry. I'm almost seventeen." Her full, red lips stimulate every salivary gland. "Do I turn you on?" she asks, grabbing the zipper tip.

"You turn lust to envy." I step forward, then back. Something inside her stomach kicks, and dies, a baby boy with a heart defect, like his mother. I push her away. "Sorry, but you're actually a little young for my taste."

"You don't like me?" She covers bare breasts with hands.

"How can you not like me?"

"You're mouthwatering, my dear." I open the door, my body weakened from hunger. "And I am sorry for your loss."

"What loss?" She slips and bangs her head against something that sounds like the sink.

I walk upstairs. The other girls whistle and cheer. "How was it?" they ask.

"Eye opening," I say, like a human who feels and cares about humans who feel and care. I brighten the overhead lights, point the girls to the mini-bar, and turn up the volume on the radio. "Drink up, ladies, and sing along if you like. That is unless you know any incantations from the past that you'd like to whisper into my ear, which I'll whisper back into yours."

"You're strange."

"And you're tantalizing."

"Where's Cindy?" they ask.

"Still in the bathroom, I assume."

"Why is your face peeling?" the unhealthiest girl asks.

"I have a skin condition."

"Is there nothing anyone can give you for it?"

"What I need you can't afford."

"Come on, girls. Let's go check on Cindy."

"Yes, please go down there and see what she's up to."

"Oh, my God," they scream from inside the bathroom. "What the fuck?"

"Ready or not, here I come," I say, sinking jagged teeth into the girl's neck who's wearing my super sex hat, then two, three, four, and five, until silence calms the echo-screams rippling across the water in the middle of a lake at the end of another gluttonous getaway.

The Way We Drive

I sat fully clothed on the edge of Christopher Buckner's bed, longing for nakedness, wanting to reach out and touch forbidden year-older skin and shiny black hair swept to the right side of a perfect skull. Square teeth. Satisfying lips. A tugging smile that nineteen years later still pulls me sideways. But I couldn't speak up, whisper please, shout yes, or swear loyalty and secrecy to whatever secrets he needed me to be loyal.

He played with silk-thin fingers a brand-name red electric guitar. My jealous heart sought ways to steal it and carry it close to my chest, to tighten it when things got loose, to pluck it when other sounds lured me away—such a tempting life. Yet all that mattered was his brand on me. He invited me to join a summer road trip to Alabama. A visit to an older sister. Two men. Two bucket seats. Side-face to side-face fact. Seven hundred and twenty miles round trip. Love and lust mingling like erupting repression. Rolling along. Forging ahead. Michael W. Smith blaring through the speakers. Amy Grant concert on September 10. Shit. College starts September 8.

"What are your plans for the fall?" I asked.

He sat quiet for a short time.

"Not sure." Voice of seventh heaven. "My dad fixes broken watches. Maybe I'll do that."

"Not interested in college?" Come with me. Share a room, stories, classes, and walks. Best friends having and doing it all. I knew exactly what I wanted.

"School isn't me."

A high school senior when we met, I didn't know the thrill of studying with him. I'd have let him cheat, no problem. Fuck every son-of-a-bitch who helped him multiply and divide, read O. Henry, sing tenor in the choir, and divvy up art supplies. Fuck every asshole who sat on the edge of his bed when I was missing. Fuck them all.

His sister in Alabama was plain, unlike his blue eyes, nothing plain about him. But if he said he loved vanilla most, then so did I.

I'd have changed anything he wanted me to change, apart from the one thing I didn't know how, or want, to change, because I believed he also possessed the change, and shouldn't he, being older, be the first to confess and open the window of hope my truth needed him to open so I could open mine and climb through, to be with him, happy on the other side. Two bona fide men living the art of realization. I can admit it now: there's nothing more damaging to lying than knowing. I saw us as old men. Years of speaking sweetly, so speak sweetly, say something raw and real to unleash my tortured tongue. Ignite the 18-me and the 19-you to talk outright about the bond growing between us inside a pickup truck sputtering to and from Alabama. Entice my lips with tenderness. Release my fingers with honesty. Impress my disbelief with conviction. Suffuse my heart's pride with sincerity. Smile whenever onlookers glanced over and saw us as a couple. A smartly pair. Youthfulness maturing into soul mates. Destiny. Fate. Textbook partners. Just as we were.

Are. Am.

"Let's switch places," he said.

"While we're driving?"

"You ever drive clutch before?"

"Clutch?" I'd never before said the word. Was that a bad thing? Did that make me less in his eyes? Did he use the word on purpose? Had I, sometime in the past, no doubt daydreaming of him, told him about my clutchlessness? "Did I tell you that?"

"No. I just figured."

"Figured how?"

"Figured you hadn't. Your cars an automatic, right?"

"Totally automatic." God, I loved driving a Ford Escort with him in the passenger seat. Going slower than necessary. Sponging up his time. Listening to Russ Taff's, Silent Love. A song for all categories of sexual expression, goddamn it.

"You ready?" he asked. "Think you can keep it in fifth gear while I take a snooze?"

"You want to go to sleep?"

"Is that a problem?"

"No." Fuck yeah, it's a problem, stay awake man, pay attention to what's happening right in front of your eyes. "Do whatever."

Our bodies intertwined. His hand pressed against my chest. His toes rubbed against my calves. His breath immersed into my neck, masculinity seducing my greediness. Then it was over. Finished. I pumped the gas pedal. He set a forehead on the passenger side window and fell asleep. Shutting me out. Yet again. Jesus, dude, I'm right here. I'm driving us in the right direction. Can't you see how far I'm willing to go for you, for me, for us? Don't you understand how much I could matter to future capabilities? This is just the beginning. We're nowhere close to the end. Tell me you feel the same. Pick me, and save me, from a life without you.

Four years at college flew by in fast semesters. I came and went during holiday breaks while he switched bookstores and heart-wrenching girlfriends. We talked a few times briefly at church, the place we had met, in the very sanctuary that said my feelings for him were banned from the Kingdom of God, bullying me to recapitulate the car trip exchange, and failing miserably. So many men's hands have been pressed against my chest, but only his left an imprint.

Courtney-Buckner Plith. Facebook Follow. March 2016. *Hi Benji. How's life?*

I'm ok. I think of u, ur hubby, and Christopher often. How is Christopher? How r u?

Christopher died in 2013 from rectal cancer. He fought hard, but God decided it was time to call him home.

Raindrops slide down the windowpane of my street-level apartment, dropping into a shallow pool that flows into the city's sewer system and races out of town.

Sleep well, Christopher Buckner. I will dream of you.

Always the Smell of
Chemistry and Aqua Net

The window shades are closed. Bobby, my husband, prefers darkness, believing transparency echoes nebulousness. He's shady, too, speaking neither of a value system nor of its usefulness. He does however understand neglect, which makes it easy for me to prove, through repetition, his truth.

I find him standing in the middle of the living room in plaid pajama bottoms and a white t-shirt dotting neon circles. He's twirling the broom like a propeller. Faster and faster. Beautiful shoulders rising and falling like the first time I saw him shirtless, first time I touched his skin, first time I knew being trapped by obsession is, and isn't, a choice. A dust storm showers the air, flecks of light falling on everything I've chosen to keep around to keep the peace.

"What's the deal, mister?"

He opens his eyes, and whispers, "This is the deal, mister."

"Are you the broom or the dust?"

"I'm the spinning." He drops the broom and takes to his knees on the hardwood floor. I sit at the kitchen table and, in my mind, pull every broken disappointment into my arms. Chest to chest, matching heartbeats, the measurement of our past, and our future, is, simply, perfect.

'TWAS THE NIGHT BEFORE
CHRISTMAS FOR HIM, TOO

The man held up a reading light, first to illuminate the red coat with white trim and then to elucidate the red pants with white trim, examining with precision the stitching on the legs, sleeves, and cuffs. A second attempt at hand sewing a Santa costume had proved both time consuming and productive. He encircled a black belt around his waist, squeezed feet into black boots, and finger-combed a white beard from Wanda's House of Hair. Then, after a long sigh, he wrapped with silver paper various size gifts and tossed them into a big, black, fleece bag. It felt right, exactly as planned. So worth the shoplifting expedition.

He turned off the fuzz-picture television and rehearsed in his mind the schedule, the route, the deliverable, and the takeaway. Last December, as he was about to leave the apartment, breaking news about two teenage boys who were caught climbing through a youth shelter window to steal Christmas gifts caused him to worry, panic, and chicken out. But this year was different. This year he was primed; nothing was going to stop him. He held a hand over the phone and picked up the receiver on the second ring, at 10pm, exactly as planned. So worth the daylong wait.

"Hey there, sis," he said, pressing the receiver into a warming ear. Latrice, his sister, who lived more than a thousand miles away in San Antonio, Texas, could be, if necessary, a time-line alibi and character witness. "Just Plexi and I this year hunkered down watching old Christmas movies." He thought the lie sounded honest. "Merry Christmas and Happy New Year, Latrice. I hope all your dreams come true next year."

He hung up the receiver, ate three Little Debbie snack cakes, and drank a glass of milk. A light snowfall crawled up the apartment windowsill while flash winds howled through barren trees in the front lot. Despite the outdoor chaos, he felt calm inside—maybe the calmest he'd ever been. Which was odd. Shouldn't he feel at least a little bit nervous? Yes, he should. But he didn't.

After rubbing three layers of white makeup on a black face—aggravated with Santa's tradition of being Caucasian—and after fingering a pair of white gloves, he looked at himself in the full length mirror—preening, twirling, authenticating. It was time to go and do what must be done. There was no other way around it. Not one.

Dozens of family, neighborhood parties of which he hadn't been invited were beginning to shut off the lights and lock the doors. The streetlights dimmed as fog rolled in, which brought him comfort. For six months he'd been practicing keeping a silhouette out of sight and out of reach. The fog was going to make it easier for him to blend in. Thanks Mother Nature. Or Buddha. Or Trolls. Or Santa.

He kissed Plexi on the forehead. "Be back soon."

Plexi let out a loud meow.

He laughed. "Just sit tight and be ready to give me one of your nine lives if I need it."

He stepped outside and readjusted two pillows sewn

into the belly of the coat. No one was stirring, not even a mouse. He smiled—damn, he loved playing this part—and tip-toed down Longview Drive to Chartreuse Way to Willow Bend Street to a fork in the road where he paused to contemplate the risks and reward of the endeavor. He could go forward or he could turn around and go home. He could change his mind. And chicken out. Again. Or he could keep going. And get what was his. The rush to satisfy hunger hit him hard, an ache mollified only by feasting. And he was starving. For his son.

Blinking Christmas lights outlined The Women's Battered Shelter's soffits. Elaborate wreaths overpowered the front doors. Candles flickering inside the lower windowsills made it difficult to not feel a little warm and cheery. His son's upper window, laced with ice and dark curtains, was reachable by rope. He flung the black bag over a shoulder and threw one end of the rope to the flattop roof. An anchor, attached to the end of the rope, hooked itself on the first try to a cement pole centering the top of the building. Merry Christmas indeed. One hand after the next, he climbed, not too bad for being forty-five and weighing two hundred and seventeen pounds. Reaching his son's window, the man paused to catch muffled breaths. He lifted the window, crawled inside, and closed like a whisper the cheap, wooden frame. At the bed, he took to his knees and mouthed the serenity prayer. Staring at the boy, he almost cried. But there was no time for tears. Nor for any sniffling noises.

"I see my kiddie's all nestled in bed."

"Santa, is that you?"

"It's just a dream, but yes it's me."

"I've been nice all year."

"Santa knows, now skootch over."

"Did you get my letter?"

"It's cold in here. Let Santa hold you."

The boy skootched over and the man laid beside him. "Tell Santa your wishes."

There was a short silence.

"I wish kids at school would stop calling me Niggalips instead of Nicolaus."

Pain ripped the man's heart as he squeezed the boy's hand. "I wish that for you, too."

They laid quiet for a very long time.

"I've got something for ya." The man sat and pulled seven gift boxes from the black bag.

The boy sat beside him and clapped without making a sound. "Are those all for me?"

"I also have a message for you from your daddy." The man kissed the boy's forehead. "He wants you to know how much he loves you. So very, very much."

"Mommy says daddy's been naughty all year long."

"He's been nice, too. You have to believe Santa on that one, okay."

"Have you been to my daddy's house yet?"

"I'll get to him later. I promise."

The boy stood and walked to the closet with thin doors that squeaked halfway open. The boy bent down and picked from the floor a small gift, wrapped in newspaper and blue duct tape. "Will you put this under my daddy's tree when you get to him?"

"Would you like to go with Santa and give it to him yourself?" The man put the boy's gift in the black bag and stood. "We can go right now, if you want."

"I can't go with you, even though you're not a stranger, but you still are one, and I'd miss mommy too much if I went with you."

"Are you sure? I can take you to your daddy's house. All you have to do is say yes."

"Mommy says daddy's house is even worse than this place."

Worse? Than this place? No. Yes. No. "I'm so sorry you have to stay here."

The boy sat on the edge of the bed and put his chin in the palms of his hands, thinking. "I'd like to see daddy, but mommy says it's better that I don't." He looked at the man. "Will you please give him the present and a big hug for me?"

"Santa could really use a helper. Sure you don't want to come with me and fly far, far away?"

"Where are the reindeer?"

"They're resting on the rooftop. So quiet, they're invisible."

"Is Rudolph's red nose invisible?"

"If you come with me, we can be invisible, too."

"Sometimes at school I pretend to be invisible. Mommy says I should be proud of who I am and not let other kids' mean words hurt me, but she doesn't go to my school so she doesn't know. She just sits in the smoking room and smokes cigarettes and says mean things about daddy."

"If you want, I can help you disappear, and then no one can hurt you."

The boy stood, quiet, thinking. "Maybe next year I can go with you, if you still want me."

"I will always want you, my son. You mustn't ever forget that, okay."

"Can I share the gifts with mommy?"

"Seven gifts for seven years are yours to do with as you see fit." The man embraced the boy and tucked him in bed. "And yes, I will give your daddy the biggest hug he's ever had. Now go to sleep and dream of kinder people and sweeter names."

"Come back next year, okay Santa. I'll probably go with you then because I'll be eight and then I won't be so scared."

"I promise to find you, wherever you are." The man

opened and closed the window, slid down the rope, and tip-toed away. At the sidewalk, he turned and blew a kiss to his son, Nicolaus, a boy without a home whose father, fucking loser, and mother, fucking liar, still doesn't (and will likely never) have court-approved stability to provide one. So worth being the evaluation of nothing.

AFTER IT ALL COMES AROUND

The apartment is ill-lit and small, each room obstructively uncomfortable with its purpose and position. The refrigerator is partway in the dining room. The bathroom shares laundry and rust linoleum duty. The front door is so close to the living room's sliding glass door, I can envision delivery people standing in confusion as to which is the main entrance and which is the most deteriorated. It's the kind of place in which people who aren't bothered by white walls, flattened carpet, and one tiny bedroom subsist. Poorly. Thank god he's hot and horny, which is all that matters. I'm not looking to move in, at least not my possessions.

"I'm into low maintenance," he says, flicking tennis shoes across black scuffmark faux wood. "People with lots of shit usually offer much the same."

I remove tennis shoes on a blue rug and stand still. Growing up, my mother said politeness waits to be invited inside and then moves with respect, even inside an ugly home.

"You coming or not?" His shirt is flung on the floor, shorts halfway down a high, curvy ass. Enticing shoulders. Scruffy beard. Gym rat. Cat tat.

That's when I see it; the one picture hanging on the wall. In the hallway. An eight by ten photo of Tyson Andrews. My ex. A man, who, because he found me in our bedroom with another man, served both a two-month moving notice and a promise to pay it forward by having sex with all sorts of men, like this man, with a name I can't recall because I didn't ask.

"Nice looking guy," I say. "He must be pretty special."

"Why's that?"

"He's the only picture on the wall."

"I forgot it was there."

"He has a sweet face."

He scoffs. "Trust me. It's an illusion."

"Is he not sweet?"

"We getting naked or what?"

"Of course. Sorry."

We do what we came to do, binging on the pieces of each other we desire to possess before ending on a high note of satisfied culmination. He's as rough as he is hung, proving what I had hoped from a first glance in the Macy's bathroom to the ten minute drive to the house. His bedroom acuity embodies spectrum sexiness, a power bottom relinquishing control, not too fast, not too slow. Experienced. Breathtaking. Raw. Rib by rib, winding down, we land on a simultaneous breathing pattern. "May I ask you a question?"

"Sure," he says, eyes closed, red cheeks, hands buried inside expanding chest hair.

"How do you know the guy in the picture?"

"He's no one."

"Was he a boyfriend?"

"He's lost and broken."

"What's his name?"

He opens his eyes and turns onto his side. "I'm telling you, he's a nobody."

"We're all somebody, aren't we?"

"Are we?" He lays on his back. "I'm not sure I believe that anymore."

"Do you not feel like a somebody?"

"It's not about feeling. It's about knowing."

We lay in silence for a short time.

"Was he a husband?"

He stands and walks to the picture, removes it, and tosses it on the bed. "There. Now it's yours. Take it. Please."

I hold the frame like a mirror and stare at a face overnight dreams continue to enunciate with care, violence, and betrayal. Experience, I've learned, impedes one's ability to disremember history. Yes, we are who we are, and yes, we are who others make us.

"He looks nothing like that, now," he says. "Talk about run down and out."

"When's the last time you saw him?"

"I don't know. A week ago. A month. Six weeks tomorrow." He sighs. "Are you always this curious about guys you don't know?"

"I'm a curious guy and I cannot lie."

We laugh.

"What are you, about thirty?" he asks.

"Thirty-seven."

"Then you must be aware of the AIDS look of the eighties and nineties."

"AIDS look?"

"You know, gaunt and lesiony, like a skeleton walking its own death."

"Does he have AIDS?"

"He says no, but I don't buy it."

"Do you have AIDS?"

"I'd have experienced at least one red flag side effect by now if I had it, right?"

"How can you be so cavalier about something so

serious?" I sit on the edge of the bed. "We just raw-dogged it and now you say you might have AIDS."

"I'm sure I don't have it." He sits on the edge of the bed. "I was tested a while back and I'm clean."

"Like one month ago, or ten, or how many?"

"Like I've got the test result around here somewhere." He walks to a small desk in the left corner of the room and opens a drawer. "Now where are you?" He turns. "And what about you? How do I know you don't have AIDS?"

"I haven't been with anyone since I split with my ex."

"And when was that?"

"A year ago yesterday."

"Was it a bad break up?"

"Aren't they all?"

He rummages the drawer, shaking ass cheeks and light brown hair. "Come out, come out, wherever you are."

I scan the room—towering piles of books and magazines with as much dust as paper. No headboard. Or baseboard. Clothes stacked in a closet without one shelf or hanger. "How long have you lived here?"

"Here it is." He lifts the paper and tosses it on the bed. "You can keep that, too."

DATE 5/10/14. PATIENT ID 4562901. PATIENT NAME MR. AGE 25. REFERRED BY PROF. DR. MAY 5. HIV ANTIBODY (AIDS TEST). RESULT: NEGATIVE.

"This test is five years old."

"Yeah. So what?"

"It's worthless. You can't rest on a five year old HIV test to know your status. You have to get tested every six months."

"Well, that's all I have, so it'll just have to do."

I toss the test result on the mattress, swallow a snap of fear, and bring the framed picture to my chest, a picture I took three years ago, on a river cruise in early August, during the exultation phase—a time when attentiveness espoused fidelity and closeness eradicated any sense of losing surplus. "I'd like to know when you took this picture."

"I didn't even want it when he gave it to me. I was like, why are you giving me a picture of you in a frame. I mean, it's not like we had a future. But since he was with this loser guy, some total slut who I told him to kick out, which I guess he eventually did, even though it killed him to do it cuz I guess this guy had a pretty rough childhood with some really fucked up parents and siblings, but because he was rich and he bought me stuff, I listened as inactively as possible without being caught." He takes a drink from a beer sitting on the nightstand and lights a cigarette. "Then he hammered a nail in the wall and hung up the picture before I could say don't, and I've just left it there ever since."

"He must have really liked you."

"I told you, man, he was old, saggy, and boring as fuck."

"Did you not like him even a little bit?"

"All I know is that I never want to look like him, I don't care how old I am." He presses the cigarette butt into an ashtray, stands, and wiggles into a pair of blue boxers. "I gotta get going. But this was fun. Maybe we can do it again sometime."

"Please tell me his name." I lift the picture. "It can't hurt to say it aloud, can it?"

"I have nothing more to say."

I dress and leave without saying goodbye, setting the picture (and HIV test) upright in the passenger seat, wondering why so many gay men travel the condomless depths of risk in order to find, hit, and ride a more titillating orgasm. Perhaps we bareback (and cheat) to proffer connection, an attempt through omission to secure affiliation, to fit in by fitting in devoid of obstruction, to bond for a moment with someone who comprehends ostracism; someone who is, and will always be, skin sameness. Or perhaps we do it in rebellion and out of spite against the majority class, majority religion, majority politics, majority intolerance who, because they're ruled by expectancies and expect others to march the same path, hate us with venom for falling so far below the world's red line of standardization. Or perhaps we do it because we're fools who believe foolishness is an action verb branded to the word, homosexual. Or perhaps we do it because it's easy, because it's risky, because it's exciting, because it's gay.

I call Tyson's cell phone number, reaching a disconnected message. I can't find him online and our old house mailbox now belongs to some Mr. and Mrs. Charles Niamo. I drive to Best Buy and purchase a camera, a Canon 20-D, just like Tyson's camera, the very one I used to take and retake his picture, and at one time put in a frame. Then I call the clinic and set up an appointment in six months for bloodwork, all kinds, top to bottom, vein and pee, wait and see, them and me.

Anything Before E. Okay F.

The idea of a relationship being based on the alphabet initially hit Eloise Udani in Body Step class at the gym, eavesdropping a conversation between two prancersizers about a preference for married name over maiden name.

"I was a T before I got married. Thank God I met an A. No more waiting in line for me."

"I was a Q who married a B, and we couldn't be happier."

"I went from V to C," the Body Step teacher chirped in. "And we've been married for twenty-one good, long years."

Each prancersizer had gone from the end of the alphabet to the beginning, Eloise thought. Perhaps that's what she needed to do.

Eloise had been married and divorced four times, unclear with each conclusion the reason for the demise. The men had complained about a lack of communication, affairs, money problems, appearance changes, and lost love, to which Eloise agreed and disagreed, although not with exactitude. There was a bigger reason why the marriages had failed, but she was never able to extrapolate the cause.

"Are you saying the key to relationship success hinges

on finding someone whose first letter of their last name is farthest away from the first letter of my maiden name?" Eloise asked the ladies.

"Absolutely," the Body Step teacher said. "What good ever comes from X, Y, and Z."

"I was always picked last," Prancer one said. "In school, for prom, for class pictures, at the DMV. But now that I'm an A, I'm always right up front and ready to be called on like a snap."

"I love being a B," Prancer two said. "There's a reason benefits starts with it."

For the next hour, as Eloise grooved, jumped, clapped, and hopped, she also recalled with growing anger Mister Sparillo, Tibbs, Yang, and Zuckerberg, ex-jerks who, like a yoyo, rolled up and unraveled down with very few tricks up their sleeve.

Later that night, after work, she logged onto the *Our Time* dating website and winked at Ted, smiled at Jarrod, said HI to Rob, and gave a thumbs up to Peter's shirtless chest and arm hair. There was no way to see last names, damn privacy filters.

Ted winked back. Jarrod added a tongue emoji to a smile. Rob said, HI CUTIE. And Peter deleted her from his message board.

Oh well. Those might not even be their real first names. In-person is better anyway. She sent a kiss to some George before clicking off and going to bed.

The next day, eager to vote for the first United States female President—Clinton—the tall man at the registration kiosk pointed her to the farthest table in the gymnasium, saying, "U through Z is all the way down there."

"You shouldn't punish people whose last names begin at the end of the alphabet," she said. "It's unfair."

"My last name's Vaughn," he said. "I had to do the same

thing."

She opened at work the staff directory and searched the last names of hot men, single or married, it didn't matter, aghast at the majority Perry. Queen. Richter. Smith. Thompson. Underwood. Valley. West. Xander. Young. Zondervan. One ugly Adolfo. Two bald Connors. Droopy Donahue. Freckle Frederickson. Gay Gaines. Halloween bowtie Hanson. And Lady Baxter. Lady Conroy. Lady Darby. Lady Fry. And Lady Kingston.

Only one hot Anderson, fired last week, according to the new semi-hot HR director, Mister Wicker. Shit.

Over the next week, she contemplated ridding men from her existence forever, until loneliness crept in and the thought of never being touched, kissed, held, and loved bruised the small part of a heart that still ticked clockwise.

The phone book was filled with Ackerman. Ballentine. Clay. Donovan. East. Foster. She sunk deep into the couch and pondered a next move. How to make last first. Where to find former rather than latter? When will it be her turn to find counterpart contentment to set free compulsive unhappiness?

The next few months held no answers, routine business distracting from making any concrete plans. Buying groceries, laundry soap, and Body Step workout gear, she whispered to herself, "Don't try so hard. Love shows up when we least expect it. Good things come to those who wait." She groaned. "Yeah, right."

Browsing the bookstore, flipping through 'The World's Most Eligible Bachelors', she bumped into a silver daddy pulling a little boy's hand.

"Sorry. Bathroom emergency," the silver daddy said with a British accent. "Interesting book you got there. May I come back and ask why?"

She laughed, and said in a fake British accent, "Good

day to you, sir, and I hope you and your companion find what you're looking for, before it's too late."

The silver daddy and the little boy disappeared. Five minutes. Ten. Fifteen. Twenty. She whispered to the book, "Good riddance, to you and yours."

Unlocking the car, she heard a British accent yell, "Hey wait."

Approaching with a jog, the silver daddy was wearing gray Puma tennis shoes, blue tight-chest Polo shirt, and green eyes so animated with color, Eloise questioned whether she'd ever before seen green.

"You didn't buy the book," he said, shifting the little boy to a left arm.

"Unadulterated rubbish," she said in the fake British accent before switching to a pirate voice. "Me thinks fifty-five dollars for a Saudi Prince be too darn expensive, matty."

"I don't think a Saudi Prince speaks pirate."

"What do you call a Saudi Prince who speaks pirate?" she asked.

He laughed. "I can honestly say, I do not know."

"Arr-rich."

"I'm Adam and this here is Adrian."

"I'm Eloise."

"It's our pleasurrrre to meet you."

"May I ask you a weird question?" she asked, sucking in her stomach.

"You mean a second weird question, don't you?"

She smiled. "What's your last name?"

"Georgie," he said. "Why do you ask?"

During the remaining days of her life, sharing each one with Adam and Adrian Georgie, she came to better understand that some people rarely get everything they want, but sometimes they get very, very close.

RINDA'S MONIKER

It's a melancholy chamber, willow wallpaper and a power-steam humidifier trying to spread calm across six pews sulking on either side of a narrow aisle leading to a white coffin sitting atop a one-step stage accommodating a wooden podium and silver microphone. An autumn-colored wreath frames a picture of death's conquest touting cat-whisker earrings, yellow teeth, perm-wild hair, and brown eyes that, although I've never seen them up close, stare beyond the camera, as if looking at something both mysterious and suspicious—me. Her skinny, little red nose declares a Caucasian commitment to the sun. A woman named Rinda Roo Hopkins, with a limp and a lisp, who broke—breaks—my heart.

"Thanks for coming," a woman says, offering a hand. "How were you acquainted?"

I stand quiet, staring at a closed coffin. The smell of new carpet and girl perfume tempts me to step back, until the woman pulls me into an embrace. "I can tell you're hurting." She squeezes. "I know it's a hard day." She exhales. "But your attendance makes me so happy."

Happy. A word with which I'm not well acquainted, rife with insinuating vagueness. A word so venerated by jolliness, the notion of both having it and not having it provokes levelheaded envy. My sister, Pam, a carbon copy of Rinda, reels my mind with jaded retrospection.

Pam and I haven't spoken for years, personalities that can't even bear Instagram pleasantries. Pam's limp came from scoliosis, and the lisp came from Father's belief that to repeatedly slap a girl across the face is to reject the embarrassing unsightliness of scoliosis. Someone should have stopped, or reported, him. Someone like Mother. Or me.

"The service will begin in a few minutes," the woman whispers, releasing me back to the room's mist. "Maybe you can say something kind about Rinda when the time comes."

I sit in the second pew on the left side. In the middle. An air duct blows heat upon my hair. The warmth brings comfort, settling my shoulders and relaxing my neck. Ex-boyfriends called me intense. Pam called me a moron. I hope someone happy sits beside me, someone who knew Rinda well and wants to stand up and say something kind, relieving me from doing, if no one else does it, what I know I won't do.

A few plaid skirts and button down suit jackets sit in the pews around me. Incoherent whispers. Tapping of shoes. Insinuations to hurry up already, we have better places to go, and be. Pam used to beg me to sit still and see what was happening right in front of my, and her, face. I never did, unwilling to let a girl, a sister, a gimp tell me what to do.

The Christian pastor follows a Christian funeral routine: prayers, scripture readings, homily, and an invitation to receive Jesus Christ as a personal savior. No one accepts the invitation. "Before we depart," he says. "Does anyone have anything else to say?"

No one answers. The woman sitting beside me whispers,

"Go ahead now. It's time."

I shake my head.

The first time I saw Rinda, she was limping to a lopsided car in a Walgreens parking lot. I called out, "Pam," waiting for my boyfriend, Daniel, now an ex-boyfriend, to finish a third shift. Daniel and I were a one-car couple with two-card appetites, downgraded from success by debt, fights, cheating, and lies—unlucky gays nail-pounding the nail-biting cliché.

I often asked Daniel about Rinda, to which he scoffed and said, "Ew." I asked what was wrong with her, to which he groaned and said, "What isn't." I asked for specifics, to which he sighed and said, "That hobble-knob-lisp is so fucking annoying. God I want her dead." I never mentioned Rinda's resemblance to Pam, fully aware that the relationship with Daniel was winding down, both of us holding on only because of an ineptitude for letting go. Pam used to say I had the attention span of a bratty toddler. Perhaps that's the reason I date bratty toddler men. After the breakup, I thought a lot about Rinda, the only reason I stayed in touch with Daniel. To know about Rinda was to care about Pam. Vicariousness at its most guilt-ridden.

"Why do you care about a woman you don't even know?" Daniel used to ask.

"There's something about her I can't let go."

"You're so fucking bizarre."

"One does project what one is."

The funeral chimes a final Amen and the woman invites me to a reception at her house three miles out of town.

"Me?"

"Yes. You."

Pam didn't attend our parent's funerals, where I stayed quiet, too. Rinda's funeral was a stadium crowd in comparison.

39

Driving up the gravel road, I see the woman sitting on a plastic chair on a porch attached to a two-story home. I'm the only car. The only visitor. OMG, it's just me and her.

"Tea?" she asks, leading indoors. The screen door, much like the wall décor, closes in with ease. Plain. Unassuming. Beige. "I made some carrot cake, if you want some. It was Rinda's favorite."

We stand like wilted sorrow in a small kitchen. Strangers linked by Rinda. But how?

"Is anyone else coming?" I take the teacup and a plate of pie to the table.

"Rinda wasn't much of a crowd pleaser." She smiles, sitting across. "Except she must have made a pretty big impression on you."

To admit to not meeting, or knowing, Rinda will likely confuse and hurt her feelings. I sip tea and nibble pie, glancing around the room as if austerity is unknown to me. The teakettle whistles, bringing my eyes back to a woman who opens and flips through a book of pictures, the first few pages announcing black and white portraits of Rinda. As a baby. Teenager. Twenty-something when she got scoliosis. Thirty-three when she got Bell's palsy. Shingles and pneumonia one month after turning forty. Irritable Bowel Syndrome at forty-one. Never married. Sweetest person in the world, but luck was not a friend. Frail as she aged. Forty-nine just last week. "God, she wanted to see fifty." She closes the book and pours tea. "Thanks for coming today. It was really nice of you."

"How do you know Rinda?" I ask.

She laughs. "Have I not introduced myself? Oh, for goodness sake. I'm Yvette, her stepsister."

"I'm Reuben."

"Like the sandwich?"

"My sister, Pam, used to call me Reuben the Cuban."

"You have a sister, too?"

"She also has scoliosis," I say.

"Did you work with Rinda at Walgreens?"

"I didn't."

"How did you know her, then?"

I should have lied about working at Walgreens. I can lie. Ask any ex-boyfriend. Or Pam. "I knew *about* her more than I actually *knew* her."

"What do you mean, knew *about* her?"

"An ex-boyfriend of mine used to work with her at Walgreens."

She squints. "What was his name?"

"Daniel."

She closes her eyes. "It's not Daniel Korn, is it?"

We sit quiet for a short time.

"Do you know him?" I ask.

Her eyes pop open. "According to Rinda, he's complete hogwash."

"How so?"

"You dated him and you're telling me you don't know why?"

Daniel Ambrose Korn. Odd name. Odder man, who didn't share feelings except about sex and the compulsion to have it. With me. Or with anyone who agreed, known more for top than bottom, negativity than objectivity, baseball than football, men than women, and bitterness than thoughtfulness. Ex number fifty-three. Another mistake I can't forget, which I blame on Rinda, who keeps me from blocking him into obliviousness.

I look up from the teacup and meet a pair of bloodshot eyes. Yvette glances at the front door before quickly turning her head away from the stained glass. Perhaps she wants me to leave, understanding my relationship with Daniel and Daniel's relationship with Rinda. Or maybe she wants me to stay, understanding that I'm the only one who came out after the funeral. Either way, she seems conflicted, tearing eyes and rubbing temples.

"Do you know what he called her at work?" she asks.

"I don't."

We sit quiet for a short time.

"How could you be with someone so cruel?" she asks. "Do you think so little of yourself?"

"What did he call her?"

"I can't say it out loud. Not this close to her death."

Hobble-knob-lisp; that's what he called Rinda. And annoying. Fucking annoying. God I want her dead. "He didn't have much of a filter. That I do know."

"I should say not." She stands and looks out the kitchen window into the backyard. "Rinda loved working at Walgreens, said everyone was so nice and funny, including the managers. She enjoyed seeing all the little kids who came in for candy and toys and things. She liked everyone there except for Daniel, who she didn't understand why he hated her so much and why he was so mean to her."

"He did have a mean streak when his buttons were pushed."

"What buttons could he have possibly possessed to make him be so skeevy?" She turns and faces me. "Was he disabled? Did he have Bell's palsy? Did he lay in a hospital bed for a month after a dozen mini strokes almost killed him?" Her tone takes on weight and height, like a mushroom cloud after explosion. "Did he? Well, did he?"

"I'm sorry he hurt her."

"Are you? I mean, how can you be when you don't even know her or know what he called her?"

"What did he call her?"

"I told you, I can't say it this close to her death."

I sit quiet, thinking about the skeevy names Daniel called me, long-winded expletives ending in piece of shit. Which didn't bother me, because I shouted them right back. Louder. Shallowness fueled by angriness. Able men able to do, and say, everything at any time, without filters. Or apologies. Or Band-Aids. Or tears.

"Before Daniel started working there, Walgreens was her favorite place in the whole world. She couldn't wait to get there. She felt needed and wanted. She felt like she belonged. Do you have any idea how hard it was for her to find that?"

"I apologize for Daniel, if it helps."

"What could you have seen in him that'd make you wanna be with someone like that? I mean, you seem sane. And kind. You definitely don't seem like someone who'd intentionally hurt a poor woman half your age for no other reason than because you're not."

I stand and push in the chair. "I think I should go."

"I'm not mad at you." She exhales. "I'm just mad that you knew him and that you didn't know what he was like or what he was doing to her while you were with him. I mean, how many other people did he hurt that you don't know about?" She pauses. "Was he cruel to you?"

"Please accept my condolences and I do thank you for the pie."

"Fine. I'll tell you, if you really wanna know."

I stop at the front door and turn around. "Honestly, I don't wanna know."

"One night Rinda heard him and some of the other employees talking about her limp and making fun of her lisp while she was in the stock room and they were outside smoking. She heard him say it'd be so funny if she tripped over the brick he was gonna put outside the door, said it'd serve her right for being such a retard. It was that very night she got a really bad fever and had a first stroke of many more to come. That was also the night she said Walgreens wasn't gonna work out, and I knew she was giving up on everything, and that there was no going back from wherever it was she was headed."

"I hope you can find it in your heart to forgive him."

"I will never forgive him. Never."

We stand quiet for a short time.

"I am glad to at least know her last name."

"You know nothing," she says, walking toward me. "Hopkins isn't her real last name. She changed it the very first week at work. No way in hell was she gonna share a name, alive or dead, with such a sick, sick man." Slamming the door behind me.

Orbital Exchange

Standing on the front porch, I throw a kiss to John and Peggy—childless like me and Lon—who live four blocks down on Wyndom Street, the better street, better yard, better house, better furnishings, better clothing, better health, better marriage, better lives, and better high school prom king and queen who Pastor Huxley called at their wedding the most fabulous couple he'd ever had the privilege to marry. At my and Lon's wedding, Pastor Huxley said, okay ya'll, good luck. But Peggy can't cook for shit. And she's a terrible host. And she and John have no flair for circulating funny one-liners and sassy, spastic zingers.

Back inside the house, clearing off the dinner table, I replay like a wake-up call the meatier portions of the table conversation, mainly a discussion about the new, American definition of marriage, the TOP 10 baby names of the year, and the twenty-eight mutually acquainted couples who have all divorced since college.

"I admire couples who know when to call it quits," Lon had said during dinner, to which I replied, "Now I know who's been removing all the batteries from the clocks."

John and Peggy laughed.

Lon stood and scoffed.

Then I said, "I'm just kidding. Jeez, Lon. Nobody cares if you have a crooked dick or that I've been seriously contemplating lesbianism."

John and Peggy howled, hunching over, grabbing their sides. That's when Lon disappeared upstairs and didn't return. Which was odd. I've said way funnier, and worse, things about his appearance. It's unclear whether John and Peggy dislike Lon, but if I were to ask a mind-reading-fortune-teller, my bet is yes, uh-huh, oh yeah.

Climbing the stairs to the bedroom, I hear Lon stirring in the spare bathroom, making noises I don't entirely understand, as he's recently claimed the space as private, locking the door and harboring himself inside like some touchy-feely-middle-aged-outlaw. Flush number four worries me. I know he's ill-tempered, but maybe he really is sick. The water faucet turns on and off, on and off, on and off.

"You okay in there?" I press an ear to the door. "You getting ready to go out somewhere?"

The fan starts to hiss.

"Hey Hey Hey." I tap three times. "It's me." I use a sweet voice, reserved for the times in life when I seek collaboration. "Knock knock."

The shower head begins to gurgle.

"You're supposed to say who's there."

He doesn't say a word.

I press my back against the door and slide down to my ass, playing the What-Could-He-Possibly-Be-Doing-Inside-Guessing-Game. When we first met, he used Dial soap for face, hair, and body. Now he uses Pantene shampoo and conditioner, H2O body wash, a blue Loofah, and Neutrogena facial soap for oily skin. Peggy refuses to believe that Lon and I used to shower together, rinsing in circle, singing, *Head and Shoulders, Knees and Toes.* Sometimes I can't believe it either. There's been no singing for years, only an absurd adeptness at taking up each other's time.

"Whatcha doing in there, cutie?"

The electric shaver hums, as does the nose and ear trimmer.

"Herrooooo in there."

"Stalking's a crime. Go away."

"It didn't come out right. Don't be mad at me for keeps."

"It came out exactly how you wanted them to hear it."

"Two days and they won't even remember it."

The hair dryer, whooshing in quick spurts, moves from low to high, high to medium, medium to low. The little hair left on his head must despise all that blowing: wild prairie grasses fighting against a tornado. There was a time when I described him as head strong and manly.

"Why do you always have to keep talking?" he asks. "Why can't you ever shut the hell up?"

I do always keep talking, and I can never shut the hell up. I'm like a rusty valve. Once I'm spun clockwise, good luck turning me back, or off. "I promise to say something negative about myself next time."

"They're not happy either."

"Fine, mister mysterious man moving methodically mamound ma mafroom." When we first met, he adored my alliteration, said it softened his rigidity and turned childhood frowns into a permanent smile. "Musy min mare much mar moo?"

"I hate it when you talk like that."

"Mah mon, moo mow moo mumit."

"No, I do not love it." The toilet lid bangs against the bowl. He blows his nose. Coughs. Clears his throat. He used to be so quiet. He never used to clear his throat. Who is this man, and more, who is he becoming?

"It sounds like a festival in there. Tell me you haven't taken up makeup and wigs?" I giggle. "You'd make one ugly drag queen."

"Leave me alone." Drawers open and close. Toiletries move from here to there. Something unrecognizable thumps across the tile countertop grout lines, like wheels rolling over rutty cracks in the highway.

"What's that noise?"

"They think they're better than us. They always have."

"Fine. What's that noise?"

The thumping stops.

"What noise?"

The shower curtain slides across the metal bar. The light underneath the door darkens.

"I could make fun of your hearing aids and your knee-length boobs," he says. "But I don't, because it's mean."

"I said I'm sorry."

He presses his back against the door and slides down. It's the closest we've been in years. His breathing turns soft. "Do you really hate my penis?"

"No. I mean, kinda. I don't know. Yeah. I guess it's a little gross."

"Have you told them that before?"

"I should have called it a faulty follicle in search of an exorcism. Now that would have been hilarious."

"They didn't seem a bit surprised when you said it."

"Peggy says bad stuff about John's body all the time, sometimes right in front of him, but he never storms off like a little kid."

"Cuz he's a pawn and Peggy knows he'll stay and take it."

"Fine. I won't mention your penis in front of them again."

"And why in the hell did you call me a spinning orbit of clipping shears?"

"I never said that."

"How day-laborer do you see me?"

I have two choices. One, admit to cluelessness and inadvertently call him a liar or two, keep him talking by playing along. "Are you naked in there?" I stick fingers underneath the door and wiggle.

He flicks water on my fingers. "The only thing that's ever been spinning around me is you."

"What was that noise?"

"You're the one who cuts everyone down and off all the time."

A spinning orbit of clipping shears does sound like something I'd say, especially about Lon in front of John and Peggy. I scroll the smartphone screen to Peggy's name, and text, *Did I say sumum bout Lon's orbit 2nite?*

Peggy usually texts back fast.

"You did cut them off pretty quick," I say.

"I didn't cut them off. I simply left out of embarrassment. Do you not see the difference?"

"Huffing off during dessert is so junior high, Lon."

"Yeah, well so is lying for fifteen years about being able to conceive." The thumping returns, this time across the tile floor. "Now leave me the fuck alone."

I sit quiet. No funny retort. No cheeky reply. No emotion beyond sad shame, both at my defective uterus and at the faceless children who float in my dreams—little ones, big ones, black ones, white ones—amorphous shapes I cannot reach, hold, savor, or love, forbid by heaven, or hell, from participating in the wild-rush-ride of motherhood, parenthood, familyhood. With Lon. I wiggle fingers underneath the door. "I didn't have a funny way to tell you that I was flawed, so I didn't tell you at all. Maybe someday you will forgive me."

His fingertips touch mine, overwhelming me with a deluge of lost enchantment our malfunctioning egos have built and our demeaning personalities have destroyed.

Peggy texts, *ur such a hoot, girl. Only ud call Lon clipping sheers. lol.*

"Lying is your orbit in case you didn't know it," he says. More dragging. "That, and pretending."

I pound the back of my head against the door. "Tell me what that noise is."

"Why did you bring up baby names tonight?"

"Peggy brought it up, not me."

"Has she ever told you why they never had children?"

"They didn't want children."

"So they could have had them, but chose not to?"

"That's the story."

Thud!

"What just fell?"

"Nothing fell."

"You wouldn't hurt yourself, Lon, would you? You'd never do anything dangerous to harm yourself, or me, right?"

He sighs, and in a hot flash of copper vividness, I see things clearly, eye to eye—every stage, every age, every heartbeat, and every bungling tale bringing to completion me and Lon.

LIFETIME GUARANTEE

9am

"I want to see my son."

"Your name isn't on the list, ma'am."

"How do you know?"

"Because there's only one person on the list, and he's a guy who shows up every day."

"Is it Michael Morris? Cuz if it is, he must know of me. All you have to do is tell him it's me, Ruth Ann, and let him know that I'm here, that I've come, that I care."

"I can't give out personal individual information."

"The patients name is Gregory Alan Horowitz and I gave birth to him. He's my DNA. How dare you keep me from seeing him?"

"Rules are rules, ma'am. I'm sorry."

"You're not sorry. Oh, wait, you are sorry. This isn't over, not by a long stretch."

10am

"Some lady named Ruth Ann came in this morning demanding to see Gregory. But I didn't let her see him."

"Was it Ruth Ann Horowitz? Oh good God. What does she want? Thanks for not letting her see him. I don't know what'd happen if he saw her."

"Is she his mother?"

"I've never met her and Gregory, when he could still talk coherently, didn't like to talk about her."

"She seems a determined woman."

"He used to say she was cruel beyond ruthless."

"Ouch."

"He used to call her that, too."

"Do you want me to call the authorities if she shows up again?"

"She's eighty-something so I'm gonna say no, that is unless she breaks the law, or a hip."

"She looks creepy in those ratty clothes, and that hair. Oh my god. Hurricane Bianca much?"

"Was she alone?"

"Who'd wanna hang out with that kind of crazy?"

"That bad, huh?"

"Yeah. That bad."

10:30am

"Hi there, hubby. How's my Gregory doing today?"

"Mymymymy."

"Today's a special day. Do you know what today is?"

"Daydaydayday."

"I like your red sweater. Very holiday glam. And I like the jingle bells on your wheelchair, too."

"Bellsbellsbellsbells."

"So handsome, you are, luvie. Did you eat breakfast?"

"Eateateateat."

"Do you want your present now or after we listen to some music?"

"Wewewewe."

"Yes, my dear, we are a we. Now stop it before I start to cry."

11am

"She's back."

"Who?"

"That Ruth Ann lady."

"Where is she?"

"Banging her hands against the nurses' desk and yelling to see him."

"Is she alone?"

"She has a cat in her hand that she keeps trying to get us to bring in here. What do you want me to do?"

"Would you mind taking her into the chapel and telling her to wait?"

"We can call the police."

"Tell her if she calms down, I'll come talk to her, but if she doesn't, I won't."

"She also brought a birth certificate. And that smell. Oh my God. It's so intense."

"Sorry for bothering you guys with this."

"We're sorry for you. Don't worry about us."

11:15am

"Listen hubby, your mom's here, and I have no clue what to do. I wish you could provide a bit of insight, just come to the surface for a second and tell me what to do."

"Mommommommom."

"Does that mean you want me to talk to her?"

"Talktalktalktalk."

"So, that's a yes?"

"Yesyesyesyes."

"Okay than. If that's what you want, that's what I'll do."

"Dodododo."

11:30am

"Is she still in the chapel?"

"She refuses to put the cat in the car and she keeps waving the birth certificate like a blowtorch."

"Of all days to make a stink, she picks Christmas."

"It's the most wonderful time of the year, don't ya know."

"So much for silent night, holy night."

"More like don we now our gay apparel."

"I'm nervous about going in there alone. Do you mind waiting outside the chapel door?"

"We're short staffed today. Sorry man. But you know I would if I could."

12:06pm

"Hello Ruth Ann."

"They won't let me see Gregory. Are you the one who put my name on the blacklist?"

"Please stay seated. I'll sit back here and you stay up there and we can just talk from these positions."

"Why do you hate me? Why did you make him hate me?"

"I don't hate you, and neither does he."

"Just how bad is he?"

"He recently got over a bad cold, but the cough won't go away."

"I saw the cold and the cough on the television, in the show about you guys."

"I wondered if any of his family would see it."

"How could I not. It's all anyone is talking about."

"It's a lot more successful than the director thought it'd be, that's for sure."

"He looks so old and I had no idea you had a beard. I'd have never known it was the two of you if your names hadn't appeared on the bottom of the screen. People told me it was Gregory, but I had to see for myself, and I felt so bad that I didn't even recognize him. That's not right. That's not the way I want it to be. That's why I'm here."

"What's up with the cat?"

"He loved cats as a boy. I thought if I brought it, it'd cheer him up and maybe he'd remember who I was and see that we had something in common."

"What's the cat's name?"

"Gregory. Like him. All I want to do is show him the cat

and see if he remembers me, remembers something about life before the."

"Before the what?"

"Before you."

"Me? Why do you hate me?"

"I hate everyone these days. Don't take it personal."

"The nurse said you brought a birth certificate."

"I figured the cat might not work so I better have a backup plan to prove I am who I say I am. I mean, prints of his baby feet are on the paper, the same feet that walked away from me to you."

"I never made him choose between us. He said it was his decision to remove himself from your."

"My what?"

"Your absentness."

12:47pm

"May I come sit beside you?"

"I'm allergic to cats, Ruth Ann."

"It's a Sphynx. See. Completely hairless. Gregory's allergic, too."

"He never told me that."

"Well, he is. And he hates pork chops and sauerkraut. Did you know that?"

"I did."

"Well, you don't know everything, even if you think you do."

"I don't think that."

"So, can I come sit beside you?"

"I think where we're sitting is fine."

"I don't bite."

"I'm not ready to be close."

"Fine, but you're worried about nothing."

"Maybe we can sit together someday, but not today."

"Look, I know how I smell, and what I look like. I'm sure I scared the staff out of their wits. But who cares about showering and doing your hair when you have a chance to see your son before it's too late. I mean, is it too late?"

"His last request before things got really bad was that he didn't want to see you under any circumstance."

"If he's as bad as the television show says, he probably won't even know who I am."

"This is hard for me, too, Ruth Ann. I want to do the right thing for all of us. But he was adamant about not wanting to see you. His exact words were, not now, not ever."

"I didn't care that he was homosexual or that he liked musicals or even that he dressed like a girl sometimes. What I cared about was keeping him safe from his brothers, who hurt him every chance they could. That's why I sent him to his grandmother. Not because I didn't want him, but because I couldn't watch over him one hundred percent of the time. Did he know that? Did he understand the motive? I tried to tell him, but I knew he wasn't listening. And then he was gone. To the world. And then to you. And I knew I'd lost the power to make that point clear. But I didn't abandon him. I saved him. At least that's what I thought I was doing at the time. Can you understand that, even a little bit?"

"All I know is that he cried whenever we talked about you, and because I didn't like to see him sad, I didn't bring you up."

"It was his brothers' fault. It wasn't mine. Yet I'm the one being punished for trying to protect him. Why am I the bad guy, the bad mom, the bad human being? Well, I'm not. I sent him away in order to keep him close. Does that not matter to anyone?"

"I honestly didn't know that."

"Well, now that you do, can I see him?"

"I'm sorry. You can't."

"I'm not the cruel one. You are. Here. Take the cat. I can't deal with it any longer. I'm an old woman and I know my time is coming up, too. But before I leave, I want to know one thing and then I'll go and I'll never come back. But you have to tell me one thing."

"I'll do my best."

"Is he a boy with you, or is he a girl?"

1:55pm

"Why won't you answer me? What are you afraid of telling me?"

"We vowed to keep our personal life discreet."

"Aren't you guys supposed to be all out and proud about your gayness?"

"We are out and we are proud."

"Then why won't you tell me?"

"Because we promised to keep it between us, and us alone."

"Well, he is a man, and the television show made it seem like he lives like a man full time so I guess I'll just have to believe that that's the truth."

"I'm sorry I can't be of better service."

"You've been of great service, if I'm seeing things correctly. Watching that television show made me thankful that he found someone, and has someone, like you. Not everyone would be so kind, taking care of someone so far along in the disease. But you do. And you care. And you've brought him here to be taken care of even better, and I seriously hope no one ever hurts him again, and I hope you'll tell him that I came to see him and that I only sent him away in order to help, not to hurt. And please set the cat in his lap and see if it brings anything back, even for a second, and here, take the birth certificate, too, keep it close, and know whenever you look at it, somewhere Gregory Alan Horowitz's mother longs to see, and hold, her son's feet."

Connect Four

A middle-aged woman, maybe a bit younger, sitting like a clump of dough in the seat to the left across the aisle, looks at me and the large, stuffed plastic bag between my feet, as if she's questioning everything she knows about men, plastic bags, and feet. Squinty. Laser-focused. Searing. I pretend obliviousness, rocking along with the noise-bump-vibrations of the train. Amtrak. Here to there. Because I have to go. Because I have to see for myself the devastation. Because I know if I don't go, I never will go, and what kind of man, knowing what I know, doesn't go?

"Christmas in July?" she asks.

I stare out the window, feigning muteness. The world whizzes by in a fast dance of blues, browns, and greens, everything morphing into cross-eyed vertigo. I tighten knees against the bag, which I refuse to put in the overhead bin. Steal the luggage, mother fuckers, but stay the hell away from the bag.

"You visiting family?" she asks.

Good god. Persistent bitch. Shut up. And go away. I know I can change seats, but I like the clean-smelling car and booger-free recliner. I turn my head and scan oil-thick hair, gravity cheeks, and eyes that radiate the same type of sadness hammering my heart. It appears that loss has come to both of us, two dozy travelers moving forward in a world offering no other choice.

"Excuse me?" I ask.

"Are those presents in the bag?"

"I guess you can call them that."

"But they're not wrapped. Why aren't they wrapped?"

"I don't know the girls who I'm giving them to."

She leans back and raises eyebrows. "Why are you giving presents to girls you don't know?"

Now that I've spoken, I realize how sometimes word-vagueness incites confusion. A grown man with a bag of presents for girls he doesn't know sounds ominous, if not potentially criminal.

"I know their mom. Knew their mom. I mean, I knew her eleven years ago."

"Knew her?" She pauses. Her eyes soften. "Is she not around anymore?"

To say yes is to confess to a finality I'm not ready to accept. To say no is a lie. Either choice leads to further conversation I'm not certain I want. But perhaps sharing is good practice. Perhaps it'll engender healing. Or perhaps it'll do nothing more than remind me of mortality, that the end is closing in on all of us.

"You okay?" she asks.

"Their mother committed suicide last Wednesday. Cops found her body in a pickup truck in the woods. Head blown off by a .44 Magnum. She was missing for two days. She has three little girls, an absent husband, no-good parents, and apparently no one to talk to."

"What was her name?"

"Daisy."

"Was she like a Daisy?"

I offer a brief smile. A full smile seems adverse to empathy. "She was a rare one. That I do remember."

"How did you know her?"

"I was twenty-one and she was ten when we met. I was home from college and learned that new neighbors had moved in next door, complete with a little face on a girl who came to the front door so full of excitement, I wondered if I'd ever known happiness. She kept coming around until I paid attention, and once I did, we started hanging out."

"What went wrong with her?"

"The little I know came from my sister, who heard it from Daisy's mom, who isn't the most coherent standard-bearer of transparency, so honestly, I don't know a lot of details."

"Do you believe she did it by, and to, herself?"

"That's what I'm told." The picture of her little hands holding a gun lowers and shakes my head. Words like hopelessness, burden, weight, energy, gunfire, and darkness derails my belief that to live in the light keeps away the darkness. "Whatever happened to her, it must have been bad."

"How old was she?"

"Twenty-one."

"And she already had three little girls?"

"Twins at eighteen and another one last year, according to Twitter."

"That's a lot of pressure to be under."

I nod. Perhaps pressure is to blame. Perhaps she disliked the pressure of being a mother? A wife? Settled? Trapped? Despair? Unhappiness?

"Do you know much about daisy, the flower?" she asks.

"Not much."

"You're in luck." She smiles. A full smile. "Because I do."

"How so?"

"I'm a weekend botanist, and my specialty is the asteraceae family, also known as the daisy family."

"Weekend botanist?"

"I couldn't afford college, but what I could afford was an encyclopedia and eventually a computer with internet service and a small garden behind a small house that's all mine." She pulls from a purse a book titled, FLOWERS. Inside the middle pages is a large white and purple flower, six pressed pedals—so real it looks fake.

"Is that a daisy?"

"It's a lily." She massages the lily and flips the pages to the back of the book. Another pressed flower appears with a dozen yellow pedals centered by a dime-size button. "This is a daisy." She hands it to me. Silk on my skin. Dead but alive. Still, but wide awake. "Is there anything in particular you'd like to know about a daisy?"

I hand the daisy back. "Is it rare?"

"It is and it isn't." She tucks the daisy in the book and closes the cover. "Like a thumbprint, each daisy is unique, even though it's part of a group of twenty-thousand species."

"What does astereceae mean?"

"Aster comes from the Greek, meaning star. Think asteroid. And also lettuce and sunflower seeds and herbal teas and medicines, which also comes from this family."

"So, a daisy is a healing agent?"

"Early colonialists used it to fight colds, yes, because it grows almost everywhere on the planet, from the polar regions to the tropics."

"Sounds like it's not very rare at all."

"I think whatever adds color to the landscape is rare indeed." She glances at the plastic bag. "What's the bag about?"

"Board games."

"Like Clue and Life?"

"More like Guess Who, Chutes and Ladders, Racko, Uno, Monopoly, and Connect Four."

"I like those games."

"These were her favorite games." The word, were, relegates my posture and taunts my determination to go forward with a feeling of utter ridiculousness. How can a board game help anyone with anything? A five or ten minute distraction at best. Cheap pieces of plastic moving around a cheap board designed to provide cheap thrills for cheap people. A book about flowers is a better gift. Or a dozen daisies sprouting from a glass vase. Or a guidebook about recovery for little girls who can't yet spell it. A goddamn kitty cat. "Her parents said she took a shine to me right away and loved whenever I came over and played board games with her, so that's what I did, sometimes for hours, often with hot cocoa, even in summer."

"You're quite fond of her, aren't you?"

"Somehow the eleven year age difference didn't matter. She was a friend and I was hers. After college, when I moved back to Minnesota, and she and her family moved to another part of town, we lost touch and I didn't think twice about her."

We sit quiet for a short time.

"Sad, huh?"

"Where's your final destination?" she asks.

"Whitefish, Montana."

"Glacier country. How beautiful."

"Seems less beautiful this trip."

"I have an idea." Her face lights up. The way Daisy's face used to light up whenever she won a board game battle. "The next stop is Cut Bank. If you want, I'll buy some wrapping paper and tape in the depot and maybe we can wrap the games together. Should have plenty of time before Whitefish."

"Where's your final destination?" I ask.

"Seattle."

"Is that where you live?"

"No. I live in Chicago now, but I have family in Seattle."

"Like parents or siblings or..."

She shakes her head. "Just a couple of girls I've known for a long time."

"How long is your visit?"

"Just a quick visit and then back on the train for home." Her voice lowers in volume, as if she's protecting it for a time in the future when she's going to need it.

"How did you know I was a terrible gift wrapper?" I ask.

She laughs. "Well, you are a man and you do seem straight."

"Do I?"

"Are you not straight?"

"Crooked as a train ride from Minneapolis to Whitefish."

"Really? I'd have never guessed."

"It's part of the reason I didn't wrap the gifts. Her husband doesn't like fags. Doesn't want me around. Calls me, in front of everyone, The Perv."

"How are you gonna get the gifts to the girls?"

"I was gonna drop them off at the front door and leave."

"But they won't know who you are, or why you gave them the games, or hear about the memories of playing them with their mother."

"I can't think of another way to do it."

She sighs. "Feels wrong, but I guess I understand."

The train stops at Cut Bank. A male voice from a speaker says, "If you step out, please stay on the platform."

"We better hurry up," she says. "Grab the bag and let's go."

Inside the depot is an invisible yellow traffic light, people pausing for others to pass before making their way ahead. Or behind. The smell of garbage and Cheerios makes me sneeze.

"What's your name?" I ask, walking beside her. "I don't know your name."

"My biblical name's Tabitha, but my friends call me Aster."

"Like in asteraceae?"

"Cute and smart. Of course you're gay." She stops in front of shelves that do not carry wrapping paper. "I should've known." She grabs a book titled *100 Ways to Be Happy*, along with a roll of tape. "This'll have to work." She pays with cash and we rush back to the train. "This is fun. Are you having fun?"

"I'm definitely having a sensation."

"And what's your name, mister non-gift wrapper?"

"I'm Devin."

She stops. "Really?" Squints. "Devin. Like Kevin. Or Evan."

"Or Heaven," I say. "What? You don't like Devin?"

"No. I do. I just figured you for something else?"

"Like who?"

We hop aboard and rest hands on legs.

"Come on." She opens the door to the bathroom, to the dressing room, and walks in. I stay outside, wondering who I look like, if not like a Devin. Did Daisy think I looked like a Devin?

"You have to come in if we're gonna wrap 'em together."

I'm frozen to the floor. I've never been in a bathroom with a woman. Not even my sister. Nor my mom. I'm nervous and sweaty. And flush.

"I won't do anything inappropriate, if that's what you're worried about." She sets the supplies on the changing table.

"Is this even allowed?"

"How old are you?" She laughs. "Get in here already."

"You sure we won't get in trouble?"

"Oh my god." She looks at the ceiling and raises both

hands. "And he's sweet, too. It's no wonder Daisy was in love with you. You make it so very, very easy."

In love. Is that what Daisy was? With me? A gay man who paid attention to a girl who became a woman who gave birth to three girls and married a man who doesn't want me around, a man who calls me, in front of everyone—poor Daisy—The Perv.

C-TAB

He's clueless to my capabilities. Which I prefer. Even a hint of awareness, beforehand, deters interaction. And arousal. Which matters a little less than it once did. Wealthy people, at least those who want to remain wealthy, rule with skepticism. Because I grew up poor, skepticism isn't a high enough bar. I've become suspicion, defense, and mistrust. In the past, during my thirties and forties, if a target of fascination knew anything about what I possessed, it was over before it began, and I was (and am) acutely proficient in snuffing out opportunists. But now that I'm fifty-five, and sick again, and now that my assets are losing worth because my body is losing property, the rules are changing. Now the target has the chance to know, and have, as much as he wants, if he'll only give me what I want, exactly as I want it.

He's the newest personal trainer at the gym, which adds credibility to his naivety, smiling as if amenability is the main reason he follows the policies and procedures of which his messy beauty is employed to practice. Rebellious hairs top a thinning coif of light black curls. A wispy beard grows on a definable jawline. Supple lips narrow as he talks from the right side of a small mouth, the left side closed as if by stitches. An image of an American cowboy, rife with bowlegged swagger, expands from long legs and emerges from brown eyes that blink as often as they abstain from making contact with anyone within his sightline. Some people might call him shy. A fixer-upper. An obscurity. A symbol of mystifying commonness. I call him an instant attraction, a man who either chooses to not see himself, or worse—hopefully for my better—disapproves of who (and what) he sees. An abandoned oak leaf? A dismantled tumbleweed? A coiled rose pedal floating adrift in buoyancy wind? Each muscle flexes potentiality. Each nod lures temptation. Each convergence is symphony orchestration playing mind-blowing, seductive, masculinity. And then he smiles, and I am poorer (and richer) in every way.

According to the gym's website, he makes eleven dollars an hour and doesn't receive health benefits, a 401K, or overtime pay. Twenty-two thousand eight hundred and eighty dollars is a pitiful yearly salary, even if he is twenty-three years old, drives a Geo Metro, and sleeps on co-workers' couches. The bald, greedy custodian, Ed, who I've used before, revealed for a crisp fifty dollar bill the trainer's age, transportation, and living arrangements. I don't know if everyone can be bought, but I do know everyone I've bought, could be bought. More, the company website states emphatically that a successful personal trainer must assemble and retain a client base within three months of employment. I've never seen him with one client. I have, however, seen him stare, squint, and crack knuckles at a computer screen, which I assume is a client database, in the personal trainer work area. Or maybe he's playing Candy Crush. All I know is that if paycheck advancement depends on customer participation, he's failing, miserably. Perhaps he too can be bought, and if so, what's the price?

I always finish exercising in the sauna, a dark room for

men who like to unwind in confined humidity. I also like the company of shirtless men in ass-merge underwear. And the chitchat. Outside the sauna, men say *sup* at best. Inside the sauna, men ramble on as if heat imports the necessary freedom to unleash the tongue. He's a sauna worshipper, too, sits on the upper bench, black earbuds attached to black cords laying like thin veins against vanilla-silk skin, sweat beads falling from the tip of an ornament nose and chin. And then he sings quietly, on key, *Right now I'm in state of mind, I wanna be in like all the time*, and I wonder if obsession is longing spiking its heart rate or is compulsion the endgame of a beginning scheme.

"I never see you with any clients."

He removes the earbuds. "What?"

"You don't have any clients. How can you make a living without any clients?"

He stares ahead, as if looking at something both unreachable and unacceptable. "Yeah. It's not as easy as they said it'd be."

"Nothing of consequence ever is."

He takes to the lower bench. "I'm Preston."

"I'm Marvin."

"So, what are you into, Marvin? Weights or cardio?"

"Cardio." The word *into* highlights an affinity for complicity.

"You should think about adding weights. It'd help your muscle tone."

"I've never been interested in my own muscle tone."

His cell phone rings. He nods and exits, as sweat beads run in fast spurts down muscle-tan legs and an immaculate back. I measure with a hand his footprints. Two hands per foot. Size twelve. Goddamn Adonis.

I dream overnight of Preston's footprints, and of his virile hands in mine leading me outside, sun streaks bouncing against carnival floats and rainbow wears as we jog to a hootenanny hayride at gay PRIDE of which I have never been, but wish to never leave. The hayride is adorned with a white canopy, glitter streamers, and a hammock—a tree house on wheels. Two speakers play love songs as multicolored flowers, which serve as a moat around the straw, blow back and forth as if in a dance of glee. We lay in the hammock, sweating, panting, and enjoying the destination of his choosing. Moreover, I am happy, a smile refracting in a compact he holds to my face to prove the look of elation. He winks, and the music fades, our hands evaporate, replacing clarity of body with fogginess of mind as I awaken to the melancholy of reality, to no hayride, to no leading, to no smiling, but to matted carpet suffocating beneath an oscillating fan blowing dust mites across the bedroom.

I stare at the ceiling for hours, wondering if Preston also enjoys popcorn, starburst chandeliers, and chocolate swirl wallpaper. The rest of the day is a litany of conjecture, surmising Preston's likes and dislikes, which is like trying to fathom the unfathomable, similar to every exam room appointment with Doctor Decay; that's what I call my doc, sometimes to his face, a man who gives empathy and statistics I don't want and advice and treatment I won't take. Not this round. Life has an expiration date, and mine, like tinnitus, is getting louder as it grows darker.

The next morning, after ten minutes of Preston-free cycling, I walk to the locker room, busy inspecting offices, hallways, tanning beds, and the pool area. I haven't yet sniffed out his scent, but I do enjoy the spoor of sweat, a mishandled gym towel, and the trajectory of burgeoning ripeness. Twinks. I like twinks. A lot.

I sit in the sauna, alone, eyes closed, for a very long time. Preston eventually opens the sauna door and takes the seat beside me. "Marvin, right?"

I nod. "So, where do you see yourself in the future, Preston? And by future, I mean three weeks from now, but also forty years from now."

He shrugs. "I've never thought about it."

Figures—youth and invincibility and all. I question whether to keep talking, and if so, about which topic. Do not mention gay. Do not mention dilated cardiomyopathy heart disease. Do not mention desperation. "I know this might sound invasive, even though it's meant to motivate vigilance, but you should work hard to improve your future every single day."

"I actually thought about what you said yesterday. About me not having any clients. How did you know that I don't have any clients?"

"I'm an observer of things that interest me."

"Three dudes have already left since I started working here and not one of 'em is doing personal training stuff. One's doing construction. One's doing the restaurant thing. And one's stalking shelves at Party City."

"How do you suppose to do it differently?" I ask, "If the typical way of doing it isn't working."

"That's what I was thinking about. Like I'm gonna have to come up with a new way to attract clients or I'm gonna be chucking lumber at Home Depot, or worse, selling balloons at Party City."

"Are you familiar with the acronym, C-TAB?" I ask.

"Like sea as in water?"

"No. Like the letter C. And the letters T, A, and B."

"What's it stand for?"

"Crises. Takeaway. Ask. Broker. It's a business model I developed for people in sales, fundraising, and brand building."

"Is that what you do for work?"

"It's what I did for work, when that kind of work

mattered."

"What do the letters do?"

"They're designed to help people build a brand from the strengths of their uniqueness."

"I'm not sure I have any those things."

"What? The strengths part or the uniqueness part?"

"Both, I guess." He lowers his voice, and his head.

"Everyone has at least one strength and one uniqueness." He lifts his head. "Is the business model hard to learn?"

"Are you familiar with Power Point?"

"Like the visual presentation on a computer?"

"Do you have email?"

"It's prestonfitnessatgmaildotcom."

"Let me attach the presentation and sent it today, if you promise to watch it." I pause, waiting for a nod, or for a yes, or for both, before proceeding.

He nods. "Yes. I will. I promise."

"I also think it's useful if we sit down afterward to discuss it."

"How long is the presentation?"

"Half an hour."

"Is it only meant for smart people?"

I soften, drawn like a circle to the vulnerability in his voice, suddenly wanting to connect him (and me) to himself: a child asking a parent for permission to proceed with a task of which the parent is adept and the child is inept, a task that requires deliberation and collaboration, the child holding the match, the parent holding the kindling, both in search of making fire.

"I didn't do so great in school," he says. "I mean, I'm not dumb, but sometimes I do have a hard time putting all the pieces together when I'm learning new concepts."

"What's one times four?"

He makes a sour face. "Four. Right?"

"Right. So, just take the four words one at a time and

you'll be fine. Trust me. You got this." My tone is both serious and temperate.

He leans forward, thinking, marinating in the sentiment. His face takes on the expressions of someone who is fluctuating between indecision, cynicism, optimism, and hope. I can almost see a thought bubble above his head, the words tumbling over each other in a fight between whether to expand the thought bubble by asking for more detail or pop the thought bubble and walk away in disdain. When he smiles and says, "I have to make this job work, so yes, I'm in," I know that he can be bought, and that I am, unilaterally, sold.

"I can't go back to before." Shakes his head. "I won't go back to before." Each word amplifies identification—whoever he was, is not who he wants to be. He wants to gain. He wants to eliminate loss, whatever it may be. We sit quiet, my mind roiling in juxtaposition: selfishness versus selflessness, give versus receive, desire versus desirability, new versus old, him versus me.

"Can you meet tomorrow at noon to go over the presentation?" I ask.

He nods. "Wanna meet at the Starbucks next to Punch Pizza on Canal Drive?"

"I prefer the Caribou by Kinko's on Wardem Street."

"Guess it's a date then," he says. "Guess I'll see ya tomorrow at noon." He leaves the sauna, waving with a right hand while closing the door with a left foot. Big fucking, captivating, delicious foot.

A date. Yes, Preston. I'm in. So very, very in. In addition, I will work with you to give you what you need in order to get from you what I want. My dear boy, I wonder, are you ready?

I dream overnight of my own heart exploding in my parents kitchen, blood splattering across white cabinets and marble floors after I confess to owning a revisionist sexual orientation, the rest of my body disintegrating amidst shrieks of disapproval, delusion, and disownment. I also dream of Preston, walking hand in hand beside me in a pink thong—laughing, dancing, kissing, modeling—at gay PRIDE.

I awaken to an erection and a fever, cooling in a glass shower and softening during a close shave. I fluff and secure my hairpiece and stand naked, cursing flabbiness inside a large closet in which I dress in Brooks tennis shoes, a dark blue Under Armor polo shirt, and Tommy Bahama shorts. Brooks bolsters comfort. Dark blue is slenderizing. Under Armor mimics a style Preston wears at the gym. And Tommy Bahama, like me, is an aging man trying through ninety-five dollar linen to smear relevance across pressing on.

Driving to Caribou, I hum the tune to *Beauty and the Beast*. Then, *I Want to Know What Love Is*. Then, *Live Like We're Dying*.

I find Preston sitting at a wooden table on the opposite side of floor-to-ceiling windows. He's dressed in checkered Vans, white shorts, and a light blue tank top revealing power arms and a meaty neck attached to unblemished skin aged for feasting. I grab the laptop and take three deep breaths, each exhale ending in Preston. Not a date. Not a date. Not a date. A mantra proffered to remind optimism the length pessimism will go to eradicate expectancy. He smiles and waves, youthfulness exaggerating eagerness, as all my fixation congeals, illness and age longing to be reborn as part of his brand.

We shake hands and euphoria speeds through my cells; the high nudges me forward, assuaging some of the fissures cigarettes and whiskey have engrained and heredity and decline have scrawled permanency onto a wearied worldview. I smile and compliment his timeliness and determination in the hope of generating, or boosting, solidarity. God, I'd love to suck him off. And eat him out. And spank him until red becomes welts and welts become a calling card we both hand over with pleasure, repeatedly.

"I got here early and saved a table. Hope this one's okay."

"It's perfect."

He stands and pulls from a front pocket, flanked by a zipper elucidating a slight bulge, a twenty-dollar bill. "Get whatever you want. I can pay." He folds the cash in half and hides it in the palm attached to lean, long fingers, crimped, as if to protect the asset from overexposure. I wonder if he went to the ATM this morning and withdrew the exact amount. Or maybe this an emergency twenty-dollar bill tucked in the most secret compartment of a brown wallet with crisscrossed leather-string veneer? I understand neither holding something of value close nor the hardship of giving it away, as I am a taker, a buyer, a shopper who will pay (and often repay) because I have a bounty of resources. I have done nothing productive with wealth, and I know, even this close to mortality, the probability of becoming attuned to philanthropic egalitarianism is as unlikely as becoming adroit at straightness. Hell, to the absolute no.

I stand ten or twelve inches taller beside him at the end of a long line leading to a peppy girl controlling the cash register area. Grooming someone in public, in a crowd, out in the open, is counter-productive to generating intimacy, instilling secrecy, and indemnifying a pact of quid pro quo. But here I am, unable to shake the amalgam of happiness, nervousness, and delight. Is this how normal people feel doing normal things in the middle of a normal day? I try not to lean too close or slump too far away, attentive instead to his swaying, like an easy breeze honing its own simulation. If he only knew how quickly I am being swept away, and how badly I wish to sweep him away with me.

We take a step forward, surrounded by surplus teens and twenties pouring in, thumbing phones, and pushing back errant strands of hair. A flash feeling of being out of touch, and out of place, hits me hard, invoking anachronisms' hissing laughter. Youth begets youth. That's the way it is. That's the way it should be. Let them have each other. Let them hang. Let them be.

"I think I'm gonna go," I say. "Sorry."

"Please don't go." Shakes his head. "I came here for you and I really want to go over the four words before I have to go to work at two. Is there anything I can do, or say, to change your mind?"

"How bad do you want this?"

"One hundred percent," he says. "Like it's all I've been thinking about lately."

Came here for you. The sentence replays in my head like a boomerang as I walk to the table, Preston's forest scent infusing every gland. Sitting across, opening the laptop, I'm enflamed by his light blue eyes staring at the screen's title page: C-TAB: Making It Work For You.

"You really do want this, don't you?"

He nods. "It's changed my entire way of thinking, and we haven't yet even discussed it."

My cell phone rings: *Doctor Decay's office.* "I should take this." I stand, walk to the men's room, and sit on the toilet lid. "This is Marvin." I look at the space between each finger, at the draining sift through which I'm losing control.

"Hello Marvin. It's Nicole, Doctor Sajjid's nurse. He wants to know if you can come in today."

"I can't today."

"How about tomorrow?"

"Just tell me what he wants."

"I just set up the appointments. I don't relay the news."

"That bad, huh?"

"When do you think you can come in?"

I close my eyes and picture Preston and I blowing bubbles during the gay PRIDE parade, embellishing the sky with messages of effervescence. "Tell doc thanks but no thanks. Tell him I'm done and goodbye."

Knock. Knock. Knock. "Marvin, are you in there? It's Preston. Is everything okay?"

I lift and drop the toilet lid and flush, making mandatory I'm-okay noises. I turn on the faucets and watch cold and hot water merge into one stream, pool near the drain, spiral round and around, and disappear with a gurgle into an unseen, untouched destination. I unlock the door and wait for something, anything, or nothing, to happen.

The door handle turns—up, down, up, down—slowly opening with a screech until Preston's head and torso pop into view. The door stops halfway from touching the wall. He scans the room, looking directly at me before looking beyond me, as if searching for something he can't see but believes he will find if he looks long enough. Nosey. Meddling. Concerned. I stand behind the door, greeting the interplay of mounting friction happening at the intersection of bringing him in or taking him out.

"You've been in here for like thirty minutes," he whispers, peaking behind his shoulder. "Are you okay?"

"Do you wanna come in?"

"Are you sick?"

"Do I look sick?" I grab his wrist and squeeze, pulling lightly his arm. "Come in quick and lock the door."

He closes the door and pushes the lock button, standing with outstretched arms. "How can I help?"

I sit on the toilet lid and stare at my shoes, counting the many steps I've taken to get to this point; a million moves, a billion revisions, a trillion lies in order to get, and have, my way.

Preston takes to his knees. "Do you need an ambulance?"

The weight of an anchor pulls my head between my knees, pinning me to every name of every man I forced on his knees, to give me what I paid for, to suck and flex and moan and slave, to beg for more and then to get it, to take the extra punishment I added—harder; wilder; tougher; nastier. Connor. Jacob. Kenneth. Nick. Scott. Wallace. James. Timothy. Benjamin. Jensen. Christopher. Lawrence. Ari. Shad. Aaron.

"Why won't you look at me?" he asks.

I sit quiet, crippled by each man's eyes, by their tears, moving me only in distance once I had finished denigrating their innocence and cheapening their significance. Many of them sobbed as I pushed them, often by foot, out the door, only to quickly rewind the web of entrapment that I repurposed and recast on novelty prey, each dispossessed of self-confidence, self-discipline, and self-love, choosing the route of transactional cash instead of pursuing the journey of permanent welfare. And I paid them well, taking everything I wanted, leaving everyone a little less human.

He leans forward. "Whatever it is, you can tell me. I just wanna be of assistance."

Being this physically close to him, I long to be closer, neither to malign nor to discard him, but to take him into my arms and to hold him, for once, as an equal partner, participant, and friend. I want to share with him more than four words inside these four walls. I want to speak freely every word from a vocabulary masked by aptitude, embarrassment, and suppression. I want to redefine the definition of beginning, middle, and end. I want to exhume, study, and restructure the origin of the start-up and the do-over. I want to reform. I want to convert. I want to confess. But we are not that couple, and I am not that hopeful.

"I'm not who I appear, Preston," I whisper. "You should go."

"But I like you. You remind me of my grandpa."

Grandpa. Of course. "Stand up. Please. You should never be on your knees for anyone."

He stands. "I was worried you might fall over and I just wanted to be able to catch you is all."

A knock on the bathroom door brings me to stand and to stare in a mirror illuminating in color all that is superficiality, shadow, and night. Preston, who stands behind in transparency and brightness, imbues my thoughts, forcing mental arbitration: should I work to crush and conquer him through a thousand nicks of belittlement and domination or should I corral and coax him into involvement through one sincere declaration.

"Please tell me what I can do to help," he says.

"What are you doing on the last Saturday of this month?"

He shrugs. "I'd have to look at my calendar, but why?"

A series of knocks rattle the door. Preston puts a hand over his mouth while I put a finger in front of my lips—a hush sign; a stay still commendation; an appeal to follow and obey. The sound of footsteps walking away allows me to open the door and to hurry out, Preston following behind like a devotee, as we walk to the table and sit. I point to the laptop screen while he pulls a twenty-dollar bill from a pocket and sets it on the table. "It's not much, but I want to give it to you for helping me."

I don't acknowledge the cash, nor do I take it. "Tell me about your grandpa."

"Well, he was smart and he also had some unique ideas about business and." He pauses, glancing at my hair. "He also wore a rug."

Rug. *How euphemistic.* "First time I got sick, lymphoma

ripped out my hair in clumps only to come back in patches."

"So, you got sick a second time, too?"

"Present."

"So, it's back?"

"It never left."

"Is that why you're being so nice to me?"

"No part of my heart is linked to altruism."

"What's altruism?"

"You should look it up. I think you'd like what you see."

"Why don't you want to tell me?"

"Because if I do, it'll only reinforce how much I'm not."

"What are you sick with?"

"An enlarged heart that's on its last leg, I'm afraid." I tap the phone in a front shirt pocket. "I was on the phone with my doc's nurse in the bathroom."

"What did the nurse say?"

"Nothing I don't already know."

"Does last leg mean you're not gonna be around much longer?"

"How about we talk about something more positive, like the presentation. Tell me what you learned."

"Okay. Sure." He scoots the chair closer to the table and clears, and swallows, throat mucus. "So the letters C-TAB is an acronym. I've heard that word before, but I didn't know what it really meant until the presentation. I also get that each letter belongs to a bullet point, and that each bullet point explains how the word works in the real world."

"Give me an example of its real world application."

"Care if I talk about how it applies to my work at the gym?" He opens a notebook filled with indecipherable handwriting, tiny words scrunched together in long sentences.

"I'd be disappointed if you didn't."

"Okay, so the crises is a client who's out of shape, let's say he has really bad heart health who wants to make some changes. The takeaway is that for a fee I can be hired to help him reach the goal. The ask is to make myself available and convince him through facts and logic that I can help make it happen, for example, maybe the money he's spending on diet fads and pain pills are better spent on a personal trainer. And the broker is me, the one who's planning, implementing, and supporting the process of change through one-on-one interaction for achievable success." He pauses, scanning the words on the page. "Am I even remotely close to getting it?"

"Not close. Spot on."

"I'm a little worried about the ask part, though," he says.

"Worried like skeptical or worried like paralysis?"

"Worried like I'm not someone who talks first, cuz I'm a bit of a word fumbler."

"You just laid out an entire business strategy and didn't word fumble once."

"Cuz I wrote it down and read it."

"You didn't word fumble the first time we talked."

"Cuz you spoke first."

"No, I didn't." Which is a lie, on purpose, fabricated to measure his reaction to disagreement and to evaluate his response to confrontation. Will he stand up with assuredness or will he wither in defeat? Testing disposition, like youth, is the subject of raising, and lowering, percentages.

"If you say it's true, then I believe it," he says, his posture withering. "I guess I don't remember it right." His voice is rutted and candid, like grafts of a thorn bush being imbedded into the stem of a sweet flower at the beginning of pollen season—unmistakably uneasy, openly decent, and inextricably bound to tradition. Whatever the accusation, he'll own it, accepting like fact the blame, which to a groomer grooming is canon, craze, and creed.

"How about we write a script for memorization and oration."

"You mean like the way a tour guide gives the same spiel to different groups."

"What I mean is to have you so well-rehearsed, you won't be able to do it any other way."

He turns a page in the notebook and pulls the pen from an ear, setting the tip on the page. "It's so cool of you to help me with this. If my grandpa was still alive, he'd be happy that I was talking business stuff with someone as successful as you."

"I do expect to be paid back in some form and fashion." I push the twenty-dollar bill into his chest. "And this isn't it."

"What could you possibly need from me?"

I point at the notebook. "May I?"

He hands it to me as if offering a gift, excitement oozing from his eyes and smile. I flip a few pages back and read, "Okay, so the crises is a client who's out of shape, let's say he has really bad heart health who wants to make some changes. The takeaway is that for a fee I can hire you to help me reach the goal. The ask is to make myself available and convince you through facts and logic that you can help make it happen, for example, maybe the money I'm spending on diet fads and pain pills are better spent on a personal trainer. And the broker is me, the one who's planning, implementing, and supporting the process of change through one-on-one interaction for achievable success." I pause, and look up. "Are you even remotely close to getting it?"

"Are you making fun of me?"

"I'm being one hundred percent serious."

"So, you wanna hire me as your personal trainer?"

"I need a personal trainer, of sorts, yes."

Preston scoots back in the chair, as if to gain, or find, perspective. "What do you mean, of sorts?"

"I mean it pays two thousand dollars. Could you use two thousand dollars?"

"Who couldn't? I mean, everyone can use that kind of money. But what's the money for?"

I scoot back in the chair, also to gain, or find, perspective. "When a client at the gym pays you to work with them, they're offering you money to do something with them, right?"

"I guess so."

"And you take their money to hang out with them, yeah?"

"Personal training doesn't cost that much money."

"The kind of personal training I need costs a bit more."

"Is this really about exercise or is it about something else?"

"I can raise the fee to two thousand five hundred dollars, if you need a more incentivized takeaway."

"You have that much money sitting around waiting to be given away?"

"Right person, right time, right scenario, rightio."

"But why me?"

If not you, then no one. "I'm not asking you to do anything illegal or anything unsafe. All I'm asking for is your time." I pause, wetting my tongue for the next revelation. "And for your body."

"What are you gonna do with my body?"

An unexpected peppering of guilt, as if I've been caught poaching, and also for the many years I engaged in poaching, gives me gooseflesh and threatens my eyes with an allergy of tears. But I do not weep, for I am not a weeper. And the guilt, much like a toupee, does not permeate substance, but sits atop a slick surface, so easily removed. Instead, I choose to give him a hint, for I am as much a hint whisperer of fantasy as I am the screaming burr of disillusion. "There is an event for which I want to hire you that takes place on Saturday, June 25th from 7am to midnight."

"You'll pay me all that money for one day of service?"

"Perhaps now you comprehend how much I value you as a client."

"Are you gonna pay the money beforehand or afterward?"

"How does half before, half after sound?"

He makes two fists and, one finger at a time, starting with the right thumb, counts in hundreds to two thousand five hundred. He finishes counting, drops the fists into a lap, and bites at a lower lip, thinking, eyes shifting north, south, east, and west, taking me on a frenetic ride of directional pontification.

"I guess half now and half later works."

I smile. "Maybe now you can buy a better car or find your own apartment."

He doesn't smile, but crosses arms across a broad, tight chest. "What exactly will we be doing?"

"A second clue costs two hundred dollars."

His shoulders droop. "Fine."

I set my wallet on the table, hundred dollar bills peeking out, grabbing his attention. I place my hands, palm down, on either side of the wallet, and whisper, "You and I will be walking around Balibee Park at gay PRIDE."

"Like gay as in homo."

"Guilty."

"But I'm not gay."

"That's the reason I'm gonna refund the two hundred dollar clue."

"So, you don't want me to be gay."

"What I want is to show you off, hand in hand, in very,

very little."

"You want us to hold hands?"

"I can make it three thousand dollars if your hands need some extra motivation."

He wrinkles his face. "By very, very little, do you mean not a lot of clothes?"

"What I mean is that if there's even a hint of yes rattling inside your brain, maybe you'll let me explain the facts and the logic of the ask, before you decide to be, or not to be, my client."

"I thought the idea was for me to get clients."

"At the gym, yes, but here, with me, no. Here, I'm the broker."

"When do you need an answer?"

"You have until the end of this conversation." I put the wallet in a front pocket. "Or until one of us gets up and walks away."

"Why can't you get someone to go with you, and do it for you, for free?"

The caution in his voice, and his ass moving to the edge of a chair, seems to require elucidation. Perhaps by laying some of it out, I'll help soothe his jitteriness and maybe even rouse enthusiasm to get, and stay, involved. Alternatively, perhaps, no matter what I say, or how I say it, he'll run away laughing, mocking me, the old queer who has no friends (or family) to walk around Lake Balibee Park at gay PRIDE.

"Okay, so here's the truth," I whisper. "I've never been to gay PRIDE, because I have never asked anyone to go, nor have I had anyone to go with, because I was too busy hiding, sexing, and lying. But my time on this roundabout gas ball is coming to a close and I realize how much I want to experience for one day a community with which I have never engaged. Not out in the open, and I know the only way I can do it is to go with someone like you, someone young, beautiful, and fresh who'll make me feel for one day a little less old, repulsive, and ruined." I pause, searching for the next, right words, ones that might mobilize the deal. "Is it a money issue? Is the fee not high enough?"

"No. Well, maybe. It's just that if you're as sick as you say you are, how do I know you'll be able to make it to the event and." He pauses, counting again with his fingers. "Is there any way you can pay all the money up front?"

"Would the decision be easier if we pretended to be Grandpa and Grandson? I mean, could you hold your grandpa's hand walking around gay PRIDE?"

He stares at the ceiling, thinking, fingers interlocked behind his head. "I did used to hold my grandpa's hand when I was little at all sorts of places."

"And you did say I resemble him."

"From 7am to midnight, you say?"

"I can make it four thousand if it'll help influence your decision."

"Is this really gonna make you happy?"

"Sometimes the realization of a dream, Preston, requires the dream person."

"How am I a dream?"

"I'll pay five thousand dollars and let you wear whatever you want, if you'll only say yes."

We sit quiet for a very long time, focused on the same thing, staring out the window at a large clock in the center of the strip mall ticking ever closer to 7am on Saturday, June 25th.

AT THE POND BETWEEN HIM AND THEM

Ettrick Bramballo had never pondered water, neither as an element nor as an environment, especially uninterested in the artificial pond resting idle sixty-feet behind the farmhouse. The pond had been a fine place for a boy to lay beside and stare at the sky on summer days, despite the ten-minute trek from the house, wading through mosquito grasses, burrs, and thistles that seemed to take pleasure in scratching legs and burrowing their bodies into the laces of tennis shoes. But Pastor Caldwell's sermon—*Get Immersed In The Water, Get Yourself Clean, and Let the Healing Flow*—had awakened in Ettrick's brain a decision: he was going to think more smartly about water, especially the water in the artificial pond, built by his father, who, like his mother, needed to get clean.

Ettrick stood at the edge of the pond and watched dirt from the edges peel into brown water. Pastor Caldwell had said that clear, clean lake water had cleansed him whole. The pond water was not clear and clean. What was Ettrick to do?

"You're the closest lake for miles," Ettrick whispered. "You'll just have to do."

The gravity of Pastor Caldwell's final sentence—*only*

when we humble ourselves before the Lord will he lift us up—
drove Ettrick to his knees. He stayed with the pond for
hours, plotting a plan to get his parents wet. And well.
And win.

Ettrick became the very next Sunday the offering plate
passer-outer, money-collector and counter, after-church
cake-distributor, card table potluck setter-upper and
taker-downer, and the Friday night bingo caller. Pastor
Caldwell often said that a commitment to God's tasks
brings an outpouring of continuous purification. Ettrick
was a believer, committed to following Pastor Caldwell's,
and God's, pathway to decontamination. Live it first; sell
it later. Lead by example, straight into the water.

"Wanna go wade in the pond?" he asked his mother.

"Fuck the pond," she said, injecting another syringe
into another vein. In front of him. No shame. No guilt. No
attempt at hiding addiction.

"Does it hurt when you do that?" he asked, choosing a
question over rebuke.

"It takes away the hurt." She threw the syringe on the
floor and leaned back in the chair. "You should try it."

"What hurt does it take away?"

"Your fourteen, Ettrick. What do you know about
hurt?"

Seven years earlier, May 1st to July 4th, 5pm to 10pm,
Ettrick and his mother watched from the living room
window his father, and his father's friend, Terry, scoop
dirt with a backhoe, slowly turning tall backyard weeds
into a sunken orifice. Guiding Ettrick's fingers, his mother
circled the pond and clapped its existence. "It may not be a
swimming pool," she said. "But it's something that's ours."
Repeating the phrase every day until his father unraveled
green garden hoses from the garage, linked the connecters,

and ran water from the well to fill the pond. "I don't know how to swim," he told his mother, who whispered, "I'll teach you, every splash along the way. And you'll love it, Ettrick, I promise. There's nothing like being in water."

When he was fourteen and a half, after his parents had separated for five months and then reunited, Ettrick asked his mother, "Why did you never swim in the pond or teach me how to swim when I was little?"

"You ask too much of me." She stumbled into the bedroom. "How can you be so selfish?" She slammed the door. "Can you not see how hard this has been on me?"

Ettrick, fifteen, unloaded his parent's troubles at the altar at church, surrendering his forehead to the warmth of Pastor Caldwell's sweaty palm and his ears to Pastor Caldwell's dry lips calling upon heaven's anointing to bestow upon Ettrick every desire of his heart. Sister Clarice and Brother Garrett also laid their hands on Ettrick, pleading with God to comfort Ettrick in his time of need. Not one of them asked for details, too busy demanding God grant Ettrick a miracle, and quoting the Bible verse, *And God will fully supply your every need according to his glorious riches in heaven.* Ettrick didn't want riches, but if it happened, okay, he'd take it.

After Ettrick stacked the Sunday school chairs and vacuumed the sanctuary, he found Pastor Caldwell standing in an office, staring out a window at the parking lot. Pastor Caldwell's shoulders were slumped, like Ettrick's father. And he was tall, too. And bald. Upon closer examination, Pastor Caldwell's sweater had a hole in it, in the back, just below the neckline.

"Need anything else before I go?"

"I have a song for ya." Pastor Caldwell held out a cassette tape. "It's track three. It's about baptism. I think it's time you partake in full submersion."

Pastor Caldwell's affirmation made Ettrick smile, though his heart grew heavy. "But my parents aren't believers. Don't they need to be saved first?"

"Listen to the song. Then decide."

"I don't have a cassette player."

Pastor Caldwell rummaged a drawer and brought out a silver cassette player. "I never use it, so keep it. Think of it as an early baptism gift."

Ettrick put the cassette tape and cassette player in a pocket. "What were you looking at through the window?"

"An empty parking lot that has always been empty."

Ettrick suddenly wished he had a driver's license and a car. "How would things be different if it was full?"

Pastor Caldwell turned around. "I think the call of God is on your life, Ettrick. Have you ever thought about being a pastor when you're older?"

Ettrick nodded. "I want to be baptized in the pond in our backyard. Can you baptize me there?"

"You can be baptized anywhere you want, as long as you believe in the sacrament and yield to the power of its transformation."

"Power of its transformation," Ettrick whispered. During chores. On the bus. At school. While his parents shot Heroin, cowering when his father brought a fist to his mother's face and screamed at her for being selfish and needy, and for using up all the drugs. At the pond, begging God to answer at least one prayer, he forwarded the cassette tape to track three and took to his knees.

Preacher pulled the boy up from the water
Alleluias rose from the banks
There was a new suit of clothes from his father
And a prayer of thanks...

Ettrick pushed stop. Enough for now. Four lines was all he could take. No clue what his father might do if he found Ettrick crying. Whenever his mother cried, his father told her to shut the fuck up.

Sundays came and went. Ettrick wished for Pastor Caldwell to mention baptism again, eager to let the healing flow. But Pastor Caldwell didn't bring it up, which confused Ettrick, who believed he had proven through good deeds and regular church attendance an ability to yield to the power of its transformation.

"I'm gonna have to sell the cows and pigs," his father said. "We need the money and besides, I don't want to do it anymore."

"But isn't that how we make money?"

"We're six months behind on everything, Ettrick. You'd know that if you'd get your mind out of the clouds of that goddamn church."

"Maybe if I got baptized in the pond, God would look upon us with favor."

His father scoffed. "God's in the abandonment business. How can you not see that?"

"Did God abandon you?"

"Leave it alone, Ettrick. You can't handle it."

"I want to clean up the pond, but I don't know how. Will you help me?"

"Fuck the pond."

"Why do you hate the pond?"

"I hate the woman who asked me to make it." His father made a fist. "Not one more word about that pond, or about God. I mean it."

"But all I want to do is make it clean."

His father's fists pummeled Ettrick's gut. "Not another word." Then he drove away, this time for two weeks.

Ettrick debated whether to talk to Pastor Caldwell about his parent's, and the farm's, deterioration. Gossip is a sin and the disclosure of family secrets was a task Ettrick wasn't sure he could accomplish without getting a sick stomach and trembling hands, like his mother's hands, and feet, darting high around the house like a trapped fly, banging against windows, trying to escape, finally lying on the couch, sometimes for days, in the same clothes, awakened by his father who threw her into a cold shower before returning, together, to their syringe addiction.

"Have you ever been baptized?" he asked his mother one morning, a rare sober morning.

"Like in water and shit?"

"Pastor Caldwell says he'll baptize me in the pond if I want. If he does, will you come watch?"

"Good god, Ettrick, why would you want to go in that gross pond? Can't you see what it's become?"

"I've asked Father how to clean it, but he won't tell, or help, me."

"You have a good heart, Ettrick." She messed up his hair. "But you're very naïve."

"Why do you hate the pond?"

"I hate the man who made it. Now go away and let me be."

Ettrick spent more time at the pond, on his knees, adding bleach, Listerine, and bright white food coloring, trying to turn malodorous filth into clear and clean. The task was pointless. Everything stayed brown. In between cleanings, he listened (and sang) the first four lines of the song, bummed to have missed eight church Sundays in a row. During the absence, he had hoped Pastor Caldwell might reach out and ask why. But he hadn't. Not even a phone call. Ettrick wondered if his church jobs had been delegated to another boy, or girl, someone with baptized parents who sat in the front row, sang loudly, tithed, lived wholesome, and said amen.

Ettrick removed shoes and socks and soaked his feet in the pond. Gotta start somewhere. The cool water tickled his toes and ankles. He pushed play, ready to hear more of the song.

The boy walked barefooted all the way home for dinner
And when they laughed at his muddy feet...

He pushed stop. Kids at school laughed at the mud beneath his fingernails and at the mud on his parents' criminal records. He was sick of mud, now that he was sixteen.

"Some pansy-voiced pastor phoned for ya," his mother said, placing dishes from the cupboard into a cardboard box. "Some Caldwell guy."

"Why are you packing the dishes?"

"You have a better way to pay for Heroin?"

"What did Pastor Caldwell say?"

"He said a bunch of stuff. Man don't know when to shut up. But he seemed excited about some evangelistical person coming to town."

Ettrick phoned the church and got the answering machine. He didn't leave a message. He'd try again. He wanted to talk to Pastor Caldwell live, to explain both the absence and the regret, to thank Pastor Caldwell again for the cassette tape and cassette player, and to find out who was doing his jobs at church. A tinge of envy wrapped itself around Ettrick's heart and pulled tight the notion of being replaced by someone holier.

What he wanted he didn't get, and what he got he didn't understand. Fuck it all, he thought, asking for forgiveness the very moment he swore.

A handmade flyer on the window of the liquor store touted Evangelist Theodore H. Skinner: August 2nd through the 5th. 7pm. Sun Grove Church. Bring a friend. Expect a miracle. Stay for the baptism service on the 5th. Ettrick smiled. He knew the 5th was a Sunday. He knew what he'd be doing on that night, sitting in the front row, ready for baptism, even if it wasn't going to take place in the backyard pond in front of his parents. No more waiting. He was seventeen. Now or never.

"Go with me to see the evangelist," he begged his mother. "Please."

"Fuck those holy rollers."

"Will you go with me?" he asked his father.

"Fuck those Bible thumpers."

It wasn't Pastor Caldwell who introduced evangelist Skinner to the crowd. It was Pastor Jacob Lyndon. A new pastor, with a nametag, stringy hair, and a big belly, a man who knew nothing of Ettrick or Ettrick's parents. Which was good. And bad. But mostly bad. The new pastor knew nothing of the cassette tape and cassette player. Nothing of the song. Nothing of the pond, which was almost empty.

"Continual sin is like beads of water spilled on the ground that cannot be gathered up because they dry too fast," the evangelist said, railing on for an hour about drug addicts, alcoholics, and the culpability of those who enable such reprehensible behavior. No mention of forgiveness, redemption, love, or baptism.

Ettrick stood, tossed the cassette tape and cassette player on the altar, and left the church. Walking barefooted a new route home to his parents, junkies strewn across the kitchen floor, foam oozing from their mouths, syringes sticking from their veins, he knew what ad to be done— turn on the cold faucet handle and watch from the sidelines water rise, drown, and cleanse the farmhouse. Whole.

WANDER-WONDER

Nighttime haze fell upon the car, headlights and radio doing much of the work, as Ernest drove from one town to the next. He didn't know where he was going, or where he was going to land, just that he had to go. Everything he owned was in the car, leaving at the house, their house, those things with which he had to disremember, although he knew he'd never be able to forget. He had a sharp mind, the one thing he liked about himself, the one thing he would never trade for an easier life, even though the idea of an easier life, especially tonight, was all-consuming.

The gas light turned on: 34 miles to empty. Lights of a town came into focus, fuzzy whites and pinks Ernest hoped might bring an inexpensive hotel with a hot tub. Or at least a big bathtub. He had bubble bath, sea salts, and oatmeal soothing cream. All he needed was a place to throw them in, lay back, and dream of life beyond reality. It'd been a rough year, the kind of year he'd suffered in childhood, over and over, alongside parents and siblings who created chaos and added to it, through unpredictability and unrest, whirlwind frenzy. Last year was the worst. Hard to believe, knowing what he knew about worst years. He had hoped adulthood might belie worse with better. But it hadn't. He had failed, which made it easy for him to believe that he was a failure.

The town presented itself in electric hues of compactness. The Stop-N-Go blinked neon cigarettes, Bud Lite, and EBT accepted here. Sitting idle in the Stop-N-Go parking lot—he'd fill the tank later—Ernest thought about ownership: a rusted Chevy Equinox; five prescription bottles filled for thirty days; three or four nice outfits; a 13-Piece Rosewood Handle Culinary Knife Set; a credit card with a $2,500 credit limit and a $200 cash advance.

As he drove to Days Inn, he thought about loss. The task was dizzying, so he stopped. Today, he thought, is all I can manage. And maybe tonight. This is my future. This is my attention span. This is what I can, and cannot, do.

The bathtub was small, so he skipped a soak and instead decided to masturbate. Twice. To images of the man who forced him to leave because the man had told him he had to go. So he left, doing what the man had ordered. Like always. This is how it had been, so this is how it had to be. Ernest pinched himself for being so accommodating to the man, fully aware that accommodation is the main reason why the man had told him to go, because the man knew Ernest was accommodating, and therefore, he'd go, leaving without tears because each one had dried up long ago. The three hundred and forty-seven mile trek had elicited one emotion: retrospect detachment. And now he was tired. So he lied down on the queen-sized bed and fell asleep, dreaming of the man's eyes, lips, and hands. He awakened at 10:47pm, phoned the front desk, and asked for the address of the local bar. He didn't ask if it was a gay bar, afraid both of the clerk's response and of the confirmation that there wasn't a gay bar for hundreds of miles. Which was fine. He only wanted to drink. He didn't want a man. A man was the last thing he wanted. But after he hung up the phone and thought about not wanting a man, he wanted a man. A real man with eyes, lips, and hands. And of course, a cock. A man to use. A man to use him. Isn't that what men do, what relationships boil down to, what life, at its most granular, is. Using and reusing each other until expiration. Yes, he thought, this is exactly what men do. And who men are.

In the lobby, he laughed at a shiny paper advertisement for Late Nite deals at Taco Bell. Which rhymes with Hell. Which is where he believed he was at, and where he was staying. He'd known a taste of heaven with the man who had forced him out. But that was yesterday, actually this morning, time ticking so fast that he was unable to remember the many times in the past when time ticked slowly with the man, especially whenever they were apart, before time brought them back together and reinstated exhilaration. Now the separation was final and time didn't mean anything save numbers turning against him. It'd be easy to call himself a pushover, bamboozled, and lost. It'd be easy to surrender to whatever anesthetizing agents hid inside life's doors, corners, and bars. It'd be easy to find a stool and drink alone. Or with someone else. Maybe he'd make a friend in this dirt road town with one stoplight blinking yellow, as if shouting go or stay, who the fuck cares.

The Lone Oak Tavern betrayed its name, packed with Badgers baseball caps, blue jean short-shorts, and four pool tables—country folk embellishing mailbox identities. The jukebox thundered 80s rock. The floorboards creaked peanut shells. The windows inched dust, black bars, and finger-streaking smoke-smudges. Home tonight, he thought, playing three songs on the jukebox: *Pour Some Sugar on Me* by Def Leppard. *Holiday* by Madonna. *Another One Bites The Dust* by Queen.

"Interesting song choices," a man behind Ernest said.

"I've never heard them played in here."

If you say so, Ernest thought, turning the bar stool, startled by the man's appearance, especially the red skin, seafoam eyes, and dry fingers holding a Bud Lite. Older than many but younger than some, like Ernest, who often lied about his age by ten years. His mother lied about her age, too. It was the Baxton thing to do. Lie and accommodate. The Baxton Way.

"You just passing through?" the man asked, stepping closer to Ernest, so close that Ernest saw nose hairs sticking from a veiny nose and sniffed beer mixed with a 90's cologne reminiscent of Drakkar. Or maybe it was Paul Sabastian. Regardless, the scent reminded him of culinary school, a decade spent trying to spray, cook, and carve away food, along with his own sexual orientation.

"I'm just here for the night."

"A whole night, wow." The man laughed. "Why here?"

Ernest hadn't prepared a response to why here. And now, staring at the man's nose, he couldn't think of any good reason. So he made up a reason. A lie. To accommodate a stranger. "I have a sister in town who has a one bedroom apartment and three dogs."

"Where in town does she live?"

The only part of town Ernest knew anything about was the Days Inn part and The Lone Oak Tavern part. He'd seen an apartment building by Days Inn. "Do you know the apartment building next to Days Inn?"

"The Commons?"

"She lives there."

"Really? I live there, too."

Shit, Ernest thought. Of course he does.

"Which floor is she on?"

"Third."

"Oh. I live on the first floor. But I've probably seen her. What does she look like and what does she drive?"

"She rarely goes outside and she doesn't drive."

"What's her last name? I'm sure I'd recognize the name from the residence list."

Anderson? Jones? Smith? Jackson? "Paulsen," Ernest said. "Constance Paulsen." After his favorite author, Gary Paulsen, and his favorite novel, Hatchet. Boy gets lost. Boy gets found. Boy gets love. Boy gets life.

"I don't recognize her name. How long has she lived there?"

Ernest wanted to change the subject. "So, what's there to do around here besides visiting a shut-in sister or hanging out at The Lone Oak?"

"This your first time in town?"

Ernest nodded. "Virgin city here."

"I'm Fred."

"I'm Ernest."

"You're a bit overdressed for the likes of The Lone Oak?"

"Am I?" Ernest scanned brown shoes, tootsie roll socks, tweed pants, Brooks Brother Oxford shirt, and a brown cashmere sweater.

"You are who you are," Fred said. "That's cool with me."

"Thanks, I guess." Was Fred flirting? No way in small town hell, even though it seemed like he was flirting. But he couldn't be. Not here. Not now. But Ernest wasn't convinced, so he decided to test the theory, to see if what he perceived about Fred was how Fred felt, albeit in the dimmest period of Ernest's life. If true, perhaps he wasn't a pushover. Bamboozled. Lost. Perhaps he was being found. Or in the process of finding.

"If I was to go to the jukebox and pick another song," Ernest said. "Tell me which one to choose."

"Pick whatever you like."

"No. You have to pick the song."

"I can't. You'll laugh at me," Fred said.

"I promise I won't."

"No one picks it. Not even me. Even though it's my favorite song from the eighties."

"Now you have to tell me," Ernest said.

Fred laughed. "Crush on You by The Jets."

"I love that song. And it's in the jukebox?"

"It was the last time I checked. But I have to be honest, I haven't checked in a while."

"If it's in there, I'm so gonna play it."

"Fine with me. Like I said, I love it."

"Why haven't you ever played it?"

"Look around. Does this look like a 'Crush On You' type of place?"

Ernest looked around, scanning middle-American people enveloped in their own spheres and agendas. He wondered if they were doing what he was doing, trying to forget the past day, the past week, the past year, so many years with a man who didn't want him anymore, who had moved on without him to another man. But who? When? Where? How? Why? He walked to the jukebox, found the song, and dropped in a quarter, unable to hear the sound of plated alloy fall into a sea of familiar company. How nice it must feel to be oneself among one's own kind. He and the man who had kicked him out had not lived lives of self-affirmation, choosing instead relegation titles such as acquaintance, roommate, single, and closet case. Not lover, partner, BFF, and openly awesome. Appeasing a world adamant at advancing labels designed to satisfy expectations. No wonder they failed as a couple. Lies doomed from the start always end an untruthful beginning. Which is what they had. And who they were. The song, Crush on You by The Jets, began to play, for Fred, who probably had a middle and last name. A feeling of being out of place hit Ernest hard. But he didn't want to leave. A hotel room is the loneliest place of all. So he stayed, turned around, and waved to Fred, who waved back and smiled, missing tooth and all.

Drink after drink, Ernest found Fred and The Lone Oak Tavern cloying, incongruity slowly shifting into acquiescence. He was here. Here was crowded. Crowded was loud. And loud is the opposite of soft. He needed loud, to help drown out the conditions of a journey laced with instability and disquietude. He had always, and never, been soft, stripped by prejudice of one and cloaked by insufficiency of the other. He was hardened in every way, standing beside off-key Fred, who was hardened, too.

"How have you survived this place?" Ernest asked.

"Unlike you, I know how to blend in."

"Do you ever wish to leave?"

"I stopped wishing for that years ago."

"Why's that?"

"Because some men are travelers and some men are not."

"Well, I can take you places, if you really wanna go somewhere."

"We can go to my truck, but that's it."

"I'll take it," Ernest whispered, leading the way to the exit sign.

Casual sex between gay men is like drinking a fruity cocktail: pick the poison, stir it up, savor the taste, pretend it'll cure the numb, order another, and push repeat. Ernest enjoyed having sex with men who understood the nuances of casual sex, especially fond of men who didn't waste time trying to redefine it.

"Cum in me," Ernest said, tapping the back of his head against the leather seat of Fred's pickup truck.

"You sure," Fred replied.

"Do it."

Fred stopped. "But you don't know me. You don't know what I do, or don't, have."

"But I know what I need."

"Do you do this often?" Fred asked.

"Hundreds of times."

Fred pulled a cock out of Ernest's ass and wiggled up jeans. "Do you really have a sister in town?"

"No."

"How old are you?"

"Twenty-eight."

"You look older."

"How old do I look?"

"You look tired," Fred whispered. "And misplaced."

Ernest laughed, and opened the door. Then he cried, and opened the door. Then he drove to Days Inn, charged another week, took a bath, swallowed pills, sharpened knives, and pretended to dial the phone number of the man who had told Ernest that he hated him and never wanted to see him again, whose last three digits ended in 911.

Bumble Bee Brouhaha

Name-calling saved me. That, and paint color. My mother taught me the former. Heaven blessed me with the latter. For many years, I believed I was less because I was poor and bi-racial. But there was a major difference between me and every other girl in the village with undressed hair and sideways teeth: my ability to see, and call, things with clarity and truth. I wasn't a mud pie or some wasted space. I was a schoolhouse maven, a library card, and a sewing machine, stitching thousands of dresses—six a week for six dollar a week—for rich, white women in town. I saved two thousand forty-eight dollars by the time I turned eighteen. I'd have stockpiled a lot more cash if my mother wasn't such a thief. Happy to leave her backstabbing cruelty behind, suitcase in hand, I walked the rutty tire tracks leading to town, whispering goodbye to every tree branch I'd climbed to look out and see if I might find myself among the pretty homes, address signs, wallpaper, bed sheets, cake plates, and bathrooms with doors in town. Which I did, erasing with efficacy the cryptic boundaries I'd placed between them and me. It was time to bring realization to Beatrice A. Muddler, and to fulfill a dream of become something of value, and maybe, just maybe, do it a little bit better than everyone else.

I found WonderPaints on a whim, answering a two-line ad in the back of the newspaper: *Are you a colorful person? If so, call 555-1453.* I phoned WonderPaints from Chip's grocery store payphone and set up an interview for the following day at 10am. Be on time. Show us your color. Wow us with snap and impress us with ingenuity. I spent twenty-five dollars on a light-blue dress and fifteen dollars on a pair of pantyhose and brown flats from Kmart. I bought from the grocery store a scrub brush and sat in the bathroom stall scrubbing grime from underneath my fingernails, trying to rid years of potting flowers and carrying shrubs on weekends for Mister Carnegie's Greenhouse.

The next morning, I got dressed in the bathroom and sprayed a bit more height in an already impressive afro. I rubbed foundation and concealer on my face and carried beneath my arm across the street a purple notepad and blue pen. I sat in the striped carpeted lobby on a brown leather chair, smiling at the peppy receptionist who introduced me to Peter, the interviewer and manager of the color-department, who nodded and said, "I disfavor people who need to be babysat or micromanaged, so I hope you're not that type."

I named him gobs-a-forehead-Peter as we walked to a glass boardroom, where I met nose-tip-to-lips-Barbara, who, before I had a chance to shake her hand or sit down, shoved in my face a hot yellow color swatch, and said, "What's the first thing that comes to your mind when you see this color?" Peter sat at the end of the table and chuckled. "So?" she asked, her voice unwaveringly uptight.

"Bumble Bee Brouhaha," I said.

"Interesting." She pulled from a leather journal a light-green color swatch. "What about this one?"

"Dollop of Zennia." I sat.

"Hmm." She brought out a shiny red color swatch.

"Conical Romance."

"Did you say conical or comical?"

"Conical. Like the shape of a cone."

"I like that name, even though I do worry conical sound too much like comical. Or conjugal. Or consequential, for that matter. What if I told you that it already has a name and that its name is Consequential Comedy? Tell me why that name does, or doesn't, work. Talk me into it. Or out of it. Just convince me through veracity."

I started to sweat. Bitch knew what she wanted, which I had to respect. "Consequential sounds negative and comedy sounds hysterical. Fuse them together and the name becomes even more unappealing. I certainly wouldn't paint a wall Consequential Comedy, but I would paint a wall Conical Romance. And why? Because conical denotes artistry, and then, by simply adding a dash of romance, it becomes all the sweeter."

"I'm almost convinced. Go on."

"Also, comedy belongs to the blue family. Dark blue in fact. For a boy's room. Or a kid's play area. Perhaps an accent wall in a pet hospital or coffee cafe. It's wrong to give a blue name to a red color."

"Conical Romance it is." She brought out a light-brown color swatch. "This one?"

"Cocoa-Bean Organza."

"Wonderful." She looked at Peter, who smiled and nodded. "Name that white wall behind Peter."

White in my life had always been the opposite of black, the summation of everything I wasn't—rich, lush, creamy, cloudy, perfect. "Cashmere Cocoon."

"Brilliant. What about the color of my skirt?"

Wacky Tacky. "Parchment Picasso."

"Terrific." She nodded at Peter, who gave two-thumbs up. "Yeah?"

"Yeah," Peter said.

"I think we're done here." She stood and pointed to the glass door. "What's your name again?"

Really? "Beatrice A. Muddler."

"Well, Beatrice A. Muddler, thanks for coming in. Do we have your phone number in case we need to get in touch with you for any reason?"

"I don't have a phone or a phone number yet but the lady at the grocery store said I could use the store's phone until I get one."

"Fine. Be sure to give the phone number to Peter before you leave."

At the receptionist's desk, Peter wrote down the phone number and we shook hands. He didn't say goodbye. Or reveal a next step. I bought at the grocery store, as a reward, a bottle of Coca Cola and then went to the library to read as many books about paint as I could read until the doors locked at 7pm. I walked outside and made my way to a park in the center of town, bathed in summertime sunlight, which, if it was a paint swatch, I'd name it Serendipitous Serenity. I slept again in the bathroom stall, hoping I was the colorful person WonderPaints was looking for, wondering how much an apartment with a real mattress and bathtub might cost, and if I could afford it.

Peter phoned the next morning. The job was mine if I was still interested. Sixteen dollars an hour. Full benefits. Nancy in Human Resources will walk through the paperwork and the employee handbook. Bring an I.D. and dress casually. "How does a start date of tomorrow at 9am sound?" Peter asked.

"See you at 8:45."

The grocery store clerk—Evelyn-the-Eavesdropper—who also owned the building, told me the apartment above the store was available to rent for five hundred a month, including gas and water. Just fill out and sign the application, give a two hundred dollar cash deposit, let out a yelp, turn the key, and step inside a one bedroom, one bath unit with hardwood floors and a dishwasher.

I set the suitcase in the middle of the living room and stared for a while out the sliding glass door at a community playground with a copper swing set, two silver slides, a green merry-go-round, and a six-rung monkey bar. I paced the apartment, planning in my head future furniture arrangements, kitchen utensils, and wall pictures splattered with all sorts of color. Every time I used the bathroom, sitting on the toilet with a lid, I got goosebumps looking at the bathtub. I'd never taken a bath. I'd only seen rich white women in full-spread color magazines take baths. Bubble baths. With a glass of champagne. Sometimes a man was on his knees finger-feeding chocolates. Sometimes the man was in the tub. Sometimes the man and woman were kissing in the tub. Tumultuous Tub Time. Fictional Fairytale. Bourgeoning Beatrice.

On the first workday, dressed in a yellow blouse, blue jeans, and green tennis shoes, I followed Peter to a white room, in which he said, "Your answers beat out fifty-two other candidates, so be proud and own it." I was ecstatic. An influx of rosy warmth and sapphire doggedness seeped into my pores. Most-Most Marvelous Me.

The first year at WonderPaints, churning like a wooden paint stick, kept my imagination busy assigning fancy names to colors that in all practical terms were violet, pink, and gray. Before WonderPaints, I called red, red. After a few months, I didn't recognize green at all. I saw Wisps-Of-Geranium, Olive-Clipperships, and Gemstonia. I strolled nature trails for inspiration. I stomped floors and banged cupboards and turned door handles for stimulation. Every spice had an alter ego color. Every piece of fabric. Every flower scent. Every car engine. Every drop of water. I named a vibrant orange Splashtacity, which sold out the very first week it hit stores. Fliptricity, its successor, sold twice as fast. And Popsacity, the final cog in the trilogy, outsold the other two in less than a month. According to Peter, not only did the series exceed expectations, but sold at an elevated pace in proximity to the overall paint-to-customer ratio within the marketing teams targeted demographic data. I loved listening to him talk. He once told Barbara and me how often his effervescent wife, Virginia, grills vegetables on the veranda. Say whatever you want, Peter, Veranda-Vegetation, and I are listening.

I had a few flops. Three to be exact. The first one was Peter's fault, pestering me to name a bluish-purple swatch after his granddaughter, Violet Iris. I still think Sivis sounds pretty. Barbara disagreed, shrugging when I told her it was also a palindrome. The CEO, turkey-neck-Barney, said it sounded like a ghastly infection in some third world country and for goodness sake, don't do it again. I may be from the grubbier part of the state (which some people do call a third world country) but I'm quite certain Vivsis doesn't exist there, at least not yet. The other two flops, which Peter mentioned in a secret meeting, were, according to Barbara, epic mistakes because of my naive misunderstanding of marginalized populations in American culture. As if I wasn't marginalized. As if I'd emigrated from Haiti or Iran. Tell me how Damsilsdykiwi is offensive to lesbians. It's the perfect way to describe pale-green. And how is Luscious-Lachica suggestive of a Latina woman's ass? It's the most befitting name for a rowdy shade of pink. It is. Two days later, Barbara fired Peter for misappropriation of funds. I was sad, wondering for a few days if I had contributed in any way to his being terminated, which I doubted. But I never asked. And I was never told. So I let it go. Some things are subjectively important and some things are not.

After my mother turned seventy-five, she decided that it was my obligation to let her move into my three bedroom rambler (with a large garden) and for me to become her give-me-no-lip custodian. As a result, I started hanging out after work—and on most weekends—in the paint sections at Wal-Mart, Sears, Home Depot, and Ace Hardware. No, my name wasn't anywhere visible (or my picture, thank God) but there I was, sitting in well-lit kiosks, row after row, for the world to see, choose, use, and love. Barbara told me, during each performance review, "Favorable public opinion is the lifeblood of business acumen." I took the statement seriously and actively listened to what the public had to say.

One September, hanging out at Mipsy's Colorama—Mipsy's a huge fan, giving me the nickname Madam Verisimilitude—I overheard two skinny, white women chatting in front of some of the color swatches. They sounded sad, not sad like they just got dumped by their husbands, but sad like they just were dumped by life.

"Jackson's Jumperjoy," the first white woman said, thumbing a cobalt swatch. "What a cute name."

"It's precious," the second white lady said. "You have to paint the room that color. You just have too."

"We actually considered naming him Jackson." She sighed. "But I guess his Jumperjoy wasn't meant to be."

"Even more reason to paint it that color." The second woman embraced the first lady. "Call it a good luck sign until the next baby comes."

"I wish paint could cover up loss. Just roll it on and be done with it forever."

"If you buy that color, I'll let you paint me, too."

"Jackson's Jumperjoy it is." The first lady laughed. "Whoever names these paint colors is a pure genius."

Pure genius. Not even my mother's invasion could ruin the joy those words painted across my heart.

Peter's replacement, violin-strings-for-hair-Renee, was a serious and quiet sort of gal, interested more in climbing the corporate ladder than providing me constructive feedback or giving me even a quarterly review, which made it easy for me to tell her, "I think it's time to retire. Twenty five years working at the same place in the same room, five days a week, eight hours a day, season after season, seems reason enough." Besides, my feet were tired. My mind was tired. And my lab coat was fraying at the hems. I was a bit surprised when Ham-hock-arms-Abby and spins-in-his-chair-Lester tied a rainbow balloon pack to the back of a chair and bought a marble sheet cake with blue frosting that read, *We'll Miss You, Beatrice,* which, if I had to name it, it'd be Rolly-Doughy-Bundt.

Yesterday was my last work day as a Senior Colorist—I do love that name—and I have to admit I was little mixed up, like ten-percent Drizzle-Drench-Plum, twenty-percent Harbor-Sill-Blue, and seventy-percent Daffodil-Combustion. I turned in my badge and decided to help Renee name a secret paint color for the companies 75th Anniversary celebration, which I won't be able to attend, because my mother needs me to drive her to yet another medical appointment, demanding bitch, relegating me to servitude rather than commendation for becoming a successful, independent woman of color. No, I won't be a twinge blue, red, or yellow, when she dies. Just black, which includes a multitude of hues and is, gradation to continuum, growing in popularity.

"Here's to a colorful way out," Renee said, lifting a golden-brown swatch. "What would you name this, Beatrice?"

"Certainly Knot," I said. "Knot with a K."

"That seems a bit harsh."

"But that's its rightful name."

"I don't think it is."

"Well, what would you name it?"

"How about Celebrational Sensation?"

"Have you ever named a paint color before?" I asked, employing a most condescending I-know-better-than-you voice, one that I'd never before used at work.

"I have an MBA from Carlson." She tipped spectacles. "And I'm also an ASID certified interior designer."

I took the swatch and shook it, trying to give us all a new perspective. Then I set it in the palm of her hand, gentle like so as not to scare or overwhelm her, and said, "What's the first thing that comes to your mind when you see this color?"

"I told you. Celebrational Sensation."

"I think you have to dig a bit deeper if you want to find a color's soul."

"A color's soul?" She sounded perplexed and upset.

"A colorist's job is to illuminate the pigment maturing beneath the skin."

"What about the name Festivity Funtime? How do you like that name?"

"If you like it, I say do it."

"Festivity Funtime it is."

I rolled back my shoulders and walked toward the exit sign. At the door, as a courtesy to WonderPaints, I turned around and said, "Perhaps it takes a life of color to name a life in color."

"Do you care to expound?"

"Certainly Not." I quietly shut the door.

Furry Foot Hand Sign

I've been the White House Easter bunny rabbit for twenty-nine years—Bush Sr., Clinton, Bush Jr., Obama. Now Trump. Supplemental weight has modified a few stitches and better designers have changed a few heads. I got the job on Christmas Eve 1988, dancing in a Christmas Tree costume for a holiday event at The Fairfax at Embassy Row hotel in Washington D.C. for President Reagan and his cabinet. Afterward, the Vice President's wife, Barbara Bush, hugging me as if we were friends, said to me in front of George Bush Sr., "He's the perfect size to be the bunny for the Easter egg hunt next spring. I want him involved. I want him hired."

One White House background check and a signature of confidentiality was all it took to get a security clearance (and pass) for one day each year. A paid gig. Plus lunch on the White House lawn and a picture with the President of the United States of America. Bush Sr. patted my back and Barbara kissed my cheeks, handing me a two thousand dollar check. Bill Clinton said well done and Hillary ignored me altogether, sending some lawyer to the entrance gate to hand me a check for three thousand dollars. Bush Jr. commented about my energy and Laura asked if the suit was hot, stuffing a check for four thousand dollars in the Easter basket. Barack Obama, who had an aide give me a six thousand dollar check before I suited up, said hola, como esta and then asked for my name during the event, while Michelle introduced me to the Obama daughters, Sasha and Malia, who stood on either side holding my hands.

Then Trump was elected.

"You're not some illegal, are you?" Trump asked, as I stood in the furry suit, holding a head in my hands, on the second floor of the White House in a room with an outdoor balcony. "And aren't you a little old to be doing this." He paused, scanning me as if I were an Easter Bunny turd. "Time for some new blood, I think. Comprende?"

I nodded. "Whatever you say."

A member of the Secret Service padded me down and looked into the hollowness of the head. "Stay out of view of the camera. This may be your day, but it has nothing to do with you. Got it?"

My fondness for the past Presidents, and their crew, solidified. "I'm a US citizen, too, ya know."

That's when I saw it. A pad of construction paper and a set of markers sitting on a coffee table in front of a gold couch. Everyone else's attention was on the Trump's, fluffing their hair, applying makeup, pressing suits and skirts, and complimenting their graciousness for hosting all the little children of the world.

I walked to the table and scribbled three words in bold red marker on a piece of white paper. I was lucky to find inside an end table a roll of tape and a ruler. I taped the ruler to the back of the construction paper and tucked it in my basket.

"Don't screw up," an aide said, more like a yell, pushing me outdoors with zip and zest.

I stood to the left of Donald Trump, waving to the

crowd with a right hand while holding the basket with a left hand. Trump welcomed the crowd, saying, "Probably this is the biggest crowd to ever attend this terrific event because no other President has done it better than me. That I can tell you."

Convinced it was my last year—and the last chance—to leave a lasting mark as the Easter bunny at the White House, I pulled out the sign and held it next to Trump's head.

I'M WITH STUPID.

Pulled by the arms inside the room and tackled by two members of the Secret Service. Pushed to the entrance gate and told, don't come back again. Ever. And don't expect one cent after that little stunt, you fucking spick. But do expect a lawsuit. Which never came, even after the video went viral and garnished eight million hits, everyone asking, *who's the person behind the mask,* which provoked a Trump tweet: That HORRIBLE easter bunny is a NOBODY UNDOCUMENTED infestation who the LOW IQ DEMS (and liar Cohen) put him up to it. Witch CAN B proven. And will B soon. Talk about COLLUSION & OBSTRUCTION. Nice! MAGA!! GO USA!!! TRUMP 2020!!!!

Yes, I was a little bummed, but not entirely surprised, when no past President, nor any Presidential relation, offered support by way of endorsement—a simple counter argument, a few words of praise, any approbation to help teach the nation (and the world) that value, distinction, worth, and reliability come in all shapes, sizes, races, and, as it is, me.

ACKNOWLEDGMENTS

The following stories were previously published in slightly different forms in the following publications:

'Dorothy Day & Hammond Night,' *Chicago Literati*
'Final Leg Home,' *Blood Puddles Literary Journal*
'The Way We Drive,' *RFD Literary Magazine*
'Always the Smell of Chemistry and Aqua Net,' *The Literary Yard*
'Twas the Night Before Christmas For Him, Too,' *Edify Fiction*
'After It All Comes Around,' *IO Literary Journal*
'Anything Before E. Okay F.,' *Gravel Literary Journal*
'Rinda's Moniker,' *Projected Letters Literary Magazine*
'Orbital Exchange,' *Weasel Press*
'Connect Four,' *Montana Mouthful Magazine*
'At The Pond Between Him and Them'* *Crack The Spine Literary Journal*
'Furry Foot Hand Sign,' *Bending Genres Lit*

*Song lyrics: *Been Through The Water*, Kyle Matthews, 'See For Yourself' Album, 2000, Benson Records, Inc. The story 'At The Pond Between Him and Them' was a nominee for the 2019 Pushcart Prize.

ABOUT SAMUEL E. COLE

It began in the countryside where fourth generation farmers tilled the hardy soil exposed in large rectangles, outlined by poplars and jack pine. The old Swedish and Norwegian accents spoke in the tinkling voices of the elder women who gathered to weave rugs by hand. The sometimes-terrifying solitude of the countryside and the beauty of a nature that would somehow spring up through a deeply frozen land profoundly formed Samuel's perspective.

Samuel E. Cole, a writer of prose and poetry, lives in Woodbury, Minnesota. His stories and poems have appeared in numerous literary magazines, including Dappled Things, Apocrypha & Abstractions, Literary Orphans, Foliate Oak, Pure Slush, Empty Sink Publishing, Breathe Free Press, Fix It Broken, A Few Lines, Second Hand Stories, Dryland Lit, Blackheart Magazine, Ascent Aspirations, The Write Launch, Garfield Lake Review, RFD Magazine, Flywheel, Dual Coast, Full of Crow, Diddledog, Rathalla Review, Image OutWrite, Storychord, Capra Review, Edify Publications, Linden Avenue Literary Journal, Subtle Fiction, The Hungry Chimera, Storgy, Queen Mob's Teahouse, Identity Theory, Literary Yard, The Bookends Review, Nixes Mate Review, Projected Letters, Montana Mouthful, Chicago Literati, Blood Puddles, Winamop, and Blink Ink.

Cole finds work in special event/development management. He's a poet, flash fiction geek, and political essayist enthusiast. His work has appeared in many literary journals, and his first poetry collection, *Bereft and the Same-Sex Heart*, was published in October 2016 by Pski's Porch Publishing. His second book, *Bloodwork*, a collection of short stories, was published by Pski's Porch Publishing in July 2017. His third book, *Siren Stitches*, a collection of short stories, winner of the J.F. Powers Prize for Short Fiction, was published by Three Waters Publishing in October 2017. A second poetry collection, Dollhouse Masquerade, was published by Truth Serum Press in May 2018. He is also an award-winning card maker and scrapbooker.

He was a finalist of the 2012 Loft Literary Center short-short story contest, a 2018 winner of the J.F. Powers Prize for Short Fiction, and is a key player in adding to the paper trail chronicles of The Minneapolis Writers Workshop. He also enjoys spending time and energy making memories with family and friends.